—— THE ——

DIVIDEND
IMPERATIVE

HOW DIVIDENDS CAN NARROW THE GAP
BETWEEN MAIN STREET AND WALL STREET

DANIEL PERIS

New York   Chicago   San Francisco   Lisbon   London   Madrid
Mexico City   Milan   New Delhi   San Juan   Seoul   Singapore   Sydney   Toronto

1 2 3 4 5 6 7 8 9 0   QFR/QFR   1 9 8 7 6 5 4 3

ISBN   978-0-07-181879-7
MHID   0-07-181879-0

e-ISBN 978-0-07-181880-3
e-MHID   0-07-181880-4

This publication is designed to provide accurate and authoritative information in regard to the subject matter covered. It is sold with the understanding that neither the author nor the publisher is engaged in rendering legal, accounting, securities trading, or other professional services. If legal advice or other expert assistance is required, the services of a competent professional person should be sought.
—*From a Declaration of Principles Jointly Adopted by a Committee of the American Bar Association and a Committee of Publishers and Associations*

The views and opinions expressed in this publication are those of the author and do not necessarily reflect the views or opinions of Federated Investors, Inc., or its affiliates.

McGraw-Hill Education books are available at special quantity discounts to use as premiums and sales promotions or for use in corporate training programs. To contact a representative, please e-mail us at bulksales@mcgraw-hill.com.

This book is printed on acid-free paper.

Still for L.A.P.

Do you know the only thing that gives me pleasure? It's to see my dividends come in.

—John D. Rockefeller

Contents

Introduction

In early 2011, I published a book—*The Strategic Dividend Investor*—that argued that investors should focus on dividends if they wanted to enjoy superior returns from their stock portfolios. At the time, the U.S. stock market had been offering investors a dividend yield (annual dividend/stock price) of 2% or less for over a decade, and the dividend payout ratio (dividends/profits) for the S&P 500 Index companies was around 30%. I pointed out that both of these figures were well below what they had been historically and what they ought to be from a financial math perspective. In that light, long-term investors would be well served to return their focus to dividend-paying and dividend-growing equities. Indeed, long-term returns were dominated by dividend payments and the growth of dividends, and dividend-focused portfolios had handily outperformed non- or low-dividend alternatives over all but the shortest measurement periods. Two years later, the situation remains little changed. If anything, as interest rates have moved even lower and the baby boomers have edged two years closer to retirement, the need for income by large swathes of the population—retirees, endowments, pension funds, etc.—has become even more pressing.

This volume builds upon the first to address a much broader and arguably a more important issue: corporate America needs to pay higher dividends. At a time when the capital markets seem to alternate between scandal (Madoff, mortgage-backed securities, insider trading) and bubble (social networking companies like Facebook, Groupon, and their ilk) and are broadly distrusted by the public, a greater focus by Wall Street on dividends rather than just share prices would be good for everyone involved. Indeed, the toggling from bubble to scandal and back again is not accidental. It is evidence of the capital markets not working as well as they might. Given that business performance is cyclical and that the humans who make up the stock market have greed and fear and emotion in abundance, the cycle of boom and bust is not likely to cease anytime soon, but a greater reliance on using the stock market as a business investment platform, rather than as a grand casino available to all, would go a long way toward tamping down that volatility. It's easy to oversell an idea, and dividend payments from large, mature, publicly traded corporations are not a panacea for all of our financial and corporate ailments. In a "back to basics" period, however, putting our investment return expectations more rather than less on a cash basis would be a substantial improvement over the current situation, which is driven almost entirely by speculation in the price of stocks rather than by the receipt of cash distributions from ongoing enterprises.

What's at stake? In 2011, it was around $480 billion. Over the past decade, it was over $3 trillion. That's the amount of money that could have been paid by S&P 500 Index companies in dividends to investors and was instead redirected elsewhere, to share repurchase programs. That's a sum large enough to interest the average investor and businessperson. But there is more to it than that. As I argue in the final chapter, what's really at stake is the trust relationship between Wall Street and Main Street. The year 2011, when *The Strategic Dividend Investor* was released, was one of protests against Wall Street excesses. The narrative of the 1% versus the 99% carried over into the 2012 presidential election. In that context, it might seem peculiar to be suggesting dividends would be part of the solution to the perceived failure of the capital markets to serve the best interests of the economy and the society at large. Or to put it another way, aren't dividends the problem, and should we really concern ourselves with what made Mr. Rockefeller happy? It may strike some as a radical notion that dividends are not the problem, but part of the solution. The abuses in the stock market, and the misperception of stocks in general, are the main culprit, not the underlying businesses that feed, house, and equip our society and employ our workforce. And it is those businesses that quite properly ought to distribute their profits in the form of dividends, not only to the Rockefellers, but also to Main Street shareholders.

Consider this then a wake-up call not only for investors, but also for corporate America, and the Wall Street that lives off both. After a 30-year drop in the dividend payout ratio— I call it here the Great Retreat—it's time for senior executives and board members to step back and clearly, soberly examine how they allocate capital and what they do with the profits that their businesses generate. This work is my contribution to that debate. It is avowedly polemical, making assertions that will be dismissed out of hand by more than a few traders, hedge fund managers, and investment bankers who like things just the way they are. So be it. Those individuals notwithstanding, the issues raised here should be top of mind for Main Street investors and high on the agenda of the company directors and officers purporting to be acting in their interests.

My argument is laid out in four sections. The first asserts the linkage between the state of a company's dividend and the value of its business. This revisits the "stocks go up because dividends go up" foundation from *The Strategic Dividend Investor.* It garnered a lot of attention, as well as some push-back, from the "buy low, sell high, repeat frequently" crowd on Wall Street. It's worth reviewing because the key element in the argument is viewing a stock as an ownership claim on an enterprise, not just a piece of (electronic) paper whose value goes up or down according to the dictates of specula-tors. Once you see a stock in that light, it is no surprise that over time the value of that business—as reflected in its share price—would rise (or fall) in line with the profit distributions coming from it. Getting to see the business behind the stock and the role of profit distributions in determining the value of a given business (and its stock) lays the groundwork for the subsequent chapters. The majority of the effort here is spent on debunking the notion that you can and should focus on the alternative notion—as Wall Street encourages you to do— of near-term earnings as the primary criterion for valuing a company. One of the oldest "earners" and dividend payers in the country—The Procter & Gamble Company—serves as the case study for this analysis. The lesson here is that inves-tors need to stop concentrating on near-term earnings, and corporate executives need to stop managing to them. This obsession with near-term earnings, rather than long-term dividends, has contributed materially to the culture of Wall Street abhorred by so many on Main Street. Stop playing games with our hard-earned money!

The second chapter focuses on the fate of the corporate cash that is currently not being distributed to company owners. Greenbacks held on the balance sheet of corporate America have been rising in recent years as cost cutting has increased profitability but caution about a slowing economy has led to lower investment back into the business that would naturally consume those dollars. As company owners, investors have every reason to expect that corporate boards will responsibly deploy that cash in the business, and that if they cannot, they would then return it to company owners as a profit-sharing check—that is, as a dividend. That goes for all companies, not just publicly traded entities. Alas, profit-sharing plans for shareholders are about the last idea that comes to mind for far too many executives of large, publicly traded corporations in this country. Instead, they believe that taking your money and putting it—get this—into the stock market, of all places, to buy the company's own shares, is equivalent to or even better than sending out a check to company owners. This section shows why the Great Retreat from dividend payments to share repurchases has been a very bad use of company cash, of your cash. Many corporate executives and "hot money" managers (who trade stocks frequently) will take strong exception to this argument. At a minimum, those in favor of the $3 trillion spent on share repurchases during the last decade will get an opportunity to defend their stance.

The third section draws on the first two to suggest that investors and corporate board members need to take a fresh look at the S&P 500 Index of large, generally mature companies, where most of the market's value is located. The index's low dividend payout ratio, around 30%, and its equally low 2% yield, reflect a fundamental mismatch between legitimate growth opportunities and the capital priorities of these corporations. Even after taking into account our country's exceptionally low interest rates (a key figure in a lot of financial equations), those yield and payout ratios rightly belong to a small business in growth mode, not to the largest businesses on the globe with long-term sales and profit growth that is a variant of U.S. GDP or, at best, global economic expansion. In short, the main part of the stock market—the companies that make up the S&P 500 Index—ought to be a dividend-distributing powerhouse, with a dividend payout ratio at the 50% or better level. It is not. Instead, it is set up for "buy low, sell high, repeat frequently" speculators. Now don't accuse me of being a spoilsport. Investors seeking "swing for the fences" opportunities may claim that encouraging the S&P 500 Index companies to pay higher dividends amounts to taking away the punch bowl just as the party heats up—to borrow a metaphor usually applied to the Federal Reserve Board and interest rates. The answer is most certainly not. There are plenty, literally thousands, of stocks of smaller companies out there with little or no dividends and potentially great growth prospects. Investors can own them as they will. I wish each and every one of you an early stake in the next eBay or Google. But let us not confuse speculation in small, high-risk, high-growth businesses with investments in the main part of the market.

The final section takes on several of the big, hot-button issues of our day—in particular the popular antipathy toward major U.S. corporations and the role that corporate boards have played in allowing the current situation to come about. I argue that the directors of the S&P 500 Index companies bear an enormous responsibility for the Great Retreat's multi-decade shift away from dividends. And in doing so, they have shown themselves to not be acting in the best interests of shareholders. They now need to lead the charge back and wrest control of the capital allocation process from empire-building CEOs and their investment banking buddies. If there is to be any meeting of the minds between Main Street and Wall Street, the boards of large corporations have to be "reborn" to practice the oversight functions that they were originally designed to perform. And if they do that, and take into consideration the reasonable investment needs of their enterprises, as well as how their excess cash has been spent in recent years, boards should and will come to the conclusion that a higher dividend payout ratio is warranted.

In addition to benefiting shareholders, a return to a cash payment system from America's largest corporations might have a chance (albeit a small one) to bridge some of the long-standing, wide gap in this country between "capital" and "labor." I want to be so bold (and readily admit to being so naive) to suggest that a renewed focus on paying dividends as the preferred profit-sharing mechanism for U.S. corporations has a positive role to play in trying to overcome the seemingly never-ending conflict in our country between organized labor and senior management. History indicates that this is a perilous task, with little chance of success, but after a century of very bad blood between these two presumed polar opposites, it is worth taking an unbiased view and suggesting that workers might be interested in a dividend-paying ownership stake in their businesses and that having everyone pulling in the same direction would attract management as well.

A shift back in the direction of cash profit distributions from major corporations to shareowners large and small won't prevent future scandals or bubbles, but on the margin, it would make the stock market less of a gambling parlor and more of a healthy, transparent platform for business investment that could and should be a good deal more trusted than it is today. Ultimately, it comes down to trust, not finance. In the current environment of mistrust, the allure of regulation (and lawsuits) is high, but without an underlying culture of responsibility and accountability (by chief executives and especially by corporate boards) and trust (on the part of Main Street shareholders), additional regulation will provide only the illusion of a healthy financial system, not the real thing.

A number of the issues raised here were mentioned, in some instances just in passing, in *The Strategic Dividend Investor*. This book should be seen as a complement to the earlier work. It is, in effect, Volume Two. While it would be helpful to familiarize yourself with that material, it is not absolutely necessary. The overlap between the two volumes is minimal by design. The one exception is the first chapter, which addresses the same key issue: looking through the stock market to see the businesses behind it. Investors cannot be reminded of the importance of this frequently enough. This work is also similar to *The Strategic Dividend Investor* in that there is enough theory—even a few math equations—to scare off some casual readers. Please do not be deterred. Read this material closely if you can; skim it if you must. But I am firmly of the belief that a basic conceptual understanding of how a complex system works positions you to have a better experience when you engage it. My purpose is not to make you into a finance expert but to get you to think like a businessperson when you approach the investment platform known as the stock market. If you run your own business, if you have an IRA or 401(k) program at work, if you own mutual funds, if you oversee your own brokerage account, dispelling some of the black-box nature of the stock market should be of use to you.

But this book has another audience: the treasurers, chief financial officers (CFOs), and board members of corporate America and their high-priced consultants. Wake up and start paying dividends. It's long overdue. A higher dividend payout ratio for the S&P 500 Index companies may not herald a strengthening economy, but the current miserly payout of many large U.S. corporations most certainly does invite a speculative environment in the markets and a hostile view toward the whole notion of stocks and the companies behind them from large parts of our society. Executives and board members need to start seeing themselves as part of the solution, not part of the problem. Encouraging corporations to pay higher dividends—the key message of this book—is the flip side of telling investors to seek higher dividends— the key message of *The Strategic Dividend Investor.* Having addressed the demand side of the equation, it is now time to nudge the suppliers. So if you are an investor in publicly traded stocks, make your voice heard to the boards of the companies in which you have a stake. You are a company owner; start acting like one.

Acknowledgments

I am once again grateful to Federated Investors, my professional home for the past decade, for granting me the latitude not only to invest client assets in the style discussed in this book but also to write about it. In particular, Walter Bean has enthusiastically supported my efforts to get the word out as to why investors should seek dividends and why large corporations should pay them. Patrick Lynch conducted numerous data runs and, in his typical fashion, analyzed them closely. Jared Hoff and Steve Crane also provided data support. Ryan Bend, Chris Donohue, Tom Donohue, John Fisher, Jim Gordon, Mike Granito, Dana Meissner, and Rob Schulte-Albert reviewed earlier drafts. Outside of Federated, David Adelman, John Heinzl, Ian Kennedy, Pierre Schell, and Jan VanEck provided constructive criticism. In several instances, the readers did not agree with specific assertions made herein, and for that reason, I am all the more appreciative of their comments. Bob Mecoy and Stephanie Frerich solved the publishing part of the equation quickly and efficiently.

1

Stocks Go Up Because Dividends Go Up

The fundamental principle which applies here is that the value of capital at any instant is derived from the value of the future income which that capital is expected to yield.

Irving Fisher, *The Nature of Capital and Income*, 1906[1]

For an institution that is supposed to offer instant and correct valuations of businesses, the U.S. stock market does a stunningly poor job of it. So says a dividend investor. And so should say any rational observer watching the market rise a few percent one day and go down by the same amount the next. How is one to navigate such a landscape? In the spirit of offering investors something beyond Wall Street's self-serving mantra of "buy low, sell high, and repeat frequently," let's review a few basics: what a business is worth, what a P/E is, why too many companies and investors focus on near-term earnings, and why that focus gets both in a muddle.

What's a Business Worth?

The conventional wisdom encourages investors to think of stocks, first and foremost, as things that are traded, go up, go down, and, if you are lucky, are bought by someone else at a much higher price than you paid for them. But what is behind those stocks? Businesses. And that's where we will start. What's a business worth? The stock market is supposed to be a means of valuing businesses, but it long ago ceased being the means and became an end unto itself. So for a moment, banish stocks from your mind and think about enterprises—large, privately held businesses, or the neighborhood dry cleaner, or your insurance agent's book of business, or the family-run chain of diners, or the local widget manufacturer, or even the company that you work for. You need not be constrained by size, by sector of the economy, or by geography. And ask yourself: how are these businesses valued?

It might help to step back and review the basic business valuation techniques online or in your long-abandoned college finance textbook. If it's your own business, think about how you regularly monitor the value of your own undertaking, what you do when you buy another business or consider offers for your own. Despite the bewildering array of methods that investors use to value stocks, business valuation comes down to a few basic concepts. The first and most basic is income—what a business or asset generates to the owner on a regular basis. That income stream and any projected growth in the payments are discounted back to the current time to determine a present value, the price you might consider fair to purchase the business. This can be dressed up in many ways, but it's really nothing more than a standard DCF (discounted cash flow) exercise. No PhD required. Despite its core simplicity, a DCF does have subjective inputs, notably the discount rate (used to come up with a present value of the future payments) and the projected growth rate of the income stream, and there are a lot of adjustments that can be made—multiple growth stages, control premiums or discounts, and so forth—but the basic math is straightforward. And consistent with that simple math, the percentage rate at which the distributions grow is what drives the change in the present value (holding the other factors equal). In short, the value of an enterprise rises in line with its distribution growth over time. If little Johnny's lawn-mowing business generates 10% more pocket cash for Johnny one summer compared to the previous one (and the higher level is sustainable and the other inputs are unchanged), the value of that business— however it is determined—should rise by the same amount. The same is true of IBM. Stocks go up (over time) because dividends go up.

But let's entertain, at least for a moment, an alternative view, that of relative valuation, which is the second major way that businesses are assessed. This approach asks what a similar asset, business, or stock has recently been bought or sold for. And there's nothing wrong with this method if the "base" enterprise has been valued properly, on an income basis. Make a few adjustments to reflect how the companies are different, and you have a reasonable estimate of worth. Alas, that is rarely the case on Wall Street. Rather, relative valuation has taken on a life of its own, with no regard for intrinsic value. It is purely relative to what a company might have sold for in the past or relative to the price of other companies.

While the seller might not care which method of valuation is being applied as long as he or she feels that the price is right, the buyer most certainly should be considering not only what other similar businesses have been valued at, but whether the intrinsic value is there—the ability of the business to generate profit distributions that, when netted back to the present time, are equal to or greater than the purchase price. Or to put it another way, paying $50,000 for a dishwashing machine may seem like a good idea if your neighbor had to pay $60,000 for the same washing machine a week ago, but it still doesn't make it a wise investment. Extend the logic to buying a tech stock in early 2000, and you get my drift. At that time, you could hear brokers extolling the virtues of some stock because it was 10% cheaper than its average, or, worse yet, selling at a 15% discount to the peer group's P/E. Fifteen percent less bad is still bad. Relative valuation is just that, relative, and limiting your analysis solely to what other people are buying is an excellent way to lose money. It is in the markets as it is in life. Doing what everyone else is doing may *explain* a poor decision, but it is no *excuse* for one. You may be able to get away with relative valuation strategies for years at a time—like riding Nasdaq stocks in the late 1990s or the financial bubble a decade later—but it doesn't make it a valid long-term strategy, even if all your friends and peers are investing the same way. Ultimately, all businesses are subject to the same rules of financial math, and those are based on cash flows to the owners. It's the same for an apartment building, a manufacturing enterprise, a professional service corporation (doctors, lawyers) or even—I daresay—a stock in a publicly traded company.

Now there are real differences between how you might value a small, local business (e.g., Johnny's lawn-mowing operation) and a global corporation (IBM) whose shares trade on the stock market. Liquidity—the ability to easily purchase or sell your stake—is something the stock market offers investors. You might not always get the price you want, but between 9:30 a.m. and 4 p.m. every business day, there are buyers and sellers of IBM in the marketplace. That is worth something. Having lots of similar companies available in the stock market probably helps, through a network effect, to raise the value of all of them. Publicly traded status also offers investors the luxury of owning part of a business without having the obligation to run it. That's worth something, too. (We'll discuss the downside of this luxury later.) On the other hand, owning a small slice of IBM means you don't control the enterprise, whereas if you buy Johnny's lawn-mowing business, you get to call the shots. My analogy has its limits, but at its heart, it is still correct: a business is a business is a business. Companies whose shares trade on public exchanges are not, by virtue of that simple fact, somehow subject to a different set of rules.

Given (mostly) free markets and the general availability of basic operating information, the prices for businesses on the stock exchanges are supposed to come pretty close to intrinsic value. Having thousands of investors doing their DCFs on a daily basis and making investment decisions accordingly should get buyers pretty close to the "right" price for a business. That is, the DCF-based valuation exercises and the relative valuation ones should end up converging and giving you a good idea of what a business, and perhaps even a stock, should sell for. This is what is believed by those who hold that the capital markets are "efficient." Alas, the reality is quite the opposite. Near-term, the market is not efficient, and the wild gyrations in stock prices make it quite clear that most investors are not doing their DCFs, or if they are, they are using wildly unrealistic assumptions such as growth rates that are too high and discount rates that are too low. (In periods of crisis, the opposite may be true—growth is underestimated and risk is rated too high.) Long term, the market has to be and is efficient, but that is small comfort for investors worried about their portfolios now.

What's a P/E?

Let's get a little closer to the relative valuation exercises that are so broadly accepted on Wall Street. In almost all instances, investors are using valuation "multiples," the price of a stock divided by some per-share figure, usually net earnings (the P/E ratio) but sometimes sales (P/S) or a version of profits called EBITDA (earnings before interest, taxes, depreciation, and amortization) for those companies where interest, taxes, depreciation, and amortization would consume most if not all of the profits. But the most widely used, by far, is the P/E multiple. So what exactly is a P/E multiple, and how does it work?

This will likely come as a surprise to most investors, but earnings multiples are just a shorthand way of expressing the key components of a DCF analysis. Bear with me while I review the math, but if you can make your way through the next few pages, you'll be better positioned to understand why you need to focus on cash distributions when you make investments. At its simplest, the P/E ratio reduces a stock's value to the inverse of the discount rate being applied to the stock's current earnings forecast out into the future.[2] Whoa— what's that actually mean? It means that if you hear that a stock has a P/E of 8, the stock is selling for 8 times current net income on a per-share basis. That P/E ratio implies that, assuming earnings stay where they are, investors are applying a 12.5% discount rate (8 = 1/0.125) to the company's future profit stream to account for the risk that those profits might not be delivered or might not be worth as much in purchasing power tomorrow as they are today. Add up all those future earnings discounted back to the present time at 12.5% per year, and they will sum to 8. That's a pretty high discount rate for the types of large, publicly traded corporations one might encounter as part of the S&P 500 Index, and that's why a major stock with a P/E of 8 is considered to be cheap.

Take a company with a P/E of 20, and it suggests that investors are using a discount rate of just 5% on that flat stream of future profits. In contrast, that is quite a low discount rate, which makes the stock expensive.

So the next time you are told that a stock is trading with a P/E of 10 or 20, you can puff out your chest, quickly do the math in your head, and opine with a definite swagger as to whether the implied discount rate is too high or too low. But do discount rates really go through the minds of investors when they are contemplating the P/E of a stock? Of course not. Investors use the P/E not as shorthand for discount rates, but as a simple measure of how expensive a stock is relative to its history and relative to other stocks. Price per share divided by profits per share. Period. Lower is better than higher, and if it must be high, let it at least be less than it has been in the past, or at least lower than the P/E of similar businesses. That's pretty much it. In an only marginally more sophisticated manner, a P/E can be viewed as a measure of a "payback" period. That is, if a stock costs $100, earns $10 per share, and has a P/E of 10, purchasers will get their money back in one decade. Lower payback periods are better than higher ones. This notion does not take into account either inflation or the rather obvious fact that what a company earns is not necessarily what the investor gets.

P/Es are convenient and allow comparison between similar entities, but, like any shortcut, they can be a little too simple. Notably, they assume flat, constant earnings into the future. Many investors believe that companies with legitimate growth potential can therefore support higher P/E ratios. But those long-term growth prospects come with a higher risk of falling short. Thus, as one factor moves up, so too would the offsetting one of the discount rate. Hence investors can employ a P/E as a simplified form of a DCF analysis and use it to compare broadly similar enterprises. In the case of close companies in one industry, say Hershey Foods (HSY) and Campbell Soup (CPB), where the growth rates and discount rates might reasonably be expected to be similar to one another, the P/E ratio is not entirely without use.

But whether stock market participants realize it or not, when using P/Es to value investments, we are back to the underlying notion of the income approach. Why is a DCF behind the P/E calculation? Because in the end, *all* financial investments have to be valued on the basis of an explicit (DCF) or an implied (P/E) cash flow analysis. There is no other way. The value of any business (or any other type of investment) is the summation of current and future income to company owners discounted to the present time. It was that way 100 years ago; it is that way now; it will be that way two centuries from now. There are other ways to value a business that may be relevant in some cases—what it would cost to replace physical assets (OK for manufacturing enterprises, not so good for brand or service businesses), contingent values based on certain circumstances such as a buyout (high discount rates), and so forth. But when looked at closely, they too end up being some variant of a DCF. Investors should take comfort from this. There is a system, and despite the fact that market participants ignore it much of the time, it does work in the long run.

The dividend discount model (DDM) is just a specific instance of a DCF where the cash flow being valued is the actual dividend received by the company owner. It's the relevant form of the DCF for large, publicly traded companies that have and distribute profits. In cases where all the cash generated is paid out to company owners as a dividend, the DCF and DDM will be identical. That is the theory. In current stock market practice, however, DCFs are used to value the profits that are in the hands of the corporate managers, not the company owners. Company owners may have a claim on those profits in a legal sense, but they do not see them except when they get their quarterly checks in the mail, assuming the company pays a dividend. But as the dividend payout ratio in this country remains stubbornly around 30%, the dividend discount model applied to a public company's declared dividend is going to yield a far smaller value than the DCF applied to all the cash being generated by the corporation overall. In theory it should not, as the 70% of the profits that are reinvested back into U.S. businesses (not paid out) are supposed to generate a higher growth rate in the future profits that are paid out as dividends. Oh, that it would. The problem is simple: that 70% left in the hands of corporate managers isn't always well spent. (We'll take up one of the biggest ways it is not well spent in a subsequent chapter.) As a consequence, the current low payout ratios that characterize many large, publicly traded U.S. corporations do not always (in fact, rarely) generate the higher dividend growth trajectory used to justify sending out such small profit-sharing checks to company owners in the first place.

And so we're back to the dividend payout ratio. Companies with legitimate growth prospects do and should reinvest some or even all of their profits—perhaps for many years—to take advantage of those growth opportunities. That is, a DDM based on a company with a low payout ratio should have a higher growth rate in the equation. But I'll just remind you again of that devilish little discount rate going up in tandem with the expected growth rate of profits. Sustaining very high rates of growth for very long periods of time is the rare exception, not the rule, despite the examples of Google (GOOG), Amazon (AMZN), and the piles of business plans sitting on the desks of venture capitalists in Silicon Valley that promise to touch all Internet users or new consumers in China and India.

At this point, you are probably asking what on earth am I going on about, and what does this have to do with the stock market? Rightly so. So let me return to the matter at hand. Investors in the stock market should value companies on the basis of DCFs of the dividends paid to company owners. They do not. Instead, they use relative valuation, most notably of earnings multiples, or P/Es. The next section takes a look at P/Es and suggests why, in their current form, they are not a very good way of valuing stocks. P/E ratios are no longer particularly useful, not because of the P part (price is there for all to see) but because the E (the supposed earnings in this simple equation) have become largely unusable.

Earnings? Which Earnings?

In claiming that dividend growth drives long-term share price appreciation, I can be charged with confusing cart and horse, and that instead, earnings drive dividends and therefore share price appreciation. Guilty as charged. If you would kindly show me which earnings horse, I'll be happy to hitch it up to the dividend cart, and we can then happily trot down the lane of asset appreciation. Now dividends are of course related to earnings—the former are paid out of the latter—so a company's earnings trajectory is relevant to what a company's ultimate dividend path will be. And over the long term, earnings and dividend patterns will be very similar. So feel free to track long-term earnings growth. And if we were conducting valuation exercises in the 1950s or even the 1970s, one could point to earnings growth and use it synonymously with dividend growth to make a point about a company's changing value to investors. But not at the present time. While the math shows clearly that the increase in the value of a business over time should and will track the growth in distributable (and distributed) profits, it's equally clear that in the near term, changes in the dividend aren't driving stock prices on most days. Those publicly traded U.S. corporations that pay a dividend generally do so four times each year, and they might change it to once a year. Stocks, including the more than half that do not pay a dividend—yes, more than half of common stocks traded in the United States with a market value above $50 million do not pay any dividend—reprice every business day, around 250 times per year.[3] Obviously something other than dividends is driving those daily share price moves. That something could be money moving into or out of the stock market (from bonds or cash), the latest bit of economic news, or something specific to individual companies. But if asked, traders and investors will say that the one thing that drives individual company share prices over time is earnings, or the perception among thousands of genuine investors and an equal or greater number of speculators as to what those earnings might be in the next quarter or year. But trying to second-guess the views of countless others may well be the lesser of the challenges facing the long-term investor seeking to understand the trajectory of the profits from which his or her dividends will be paid. The far greater challenge is just figuring out which earnings figure to use.

Let me outline the problems with "earnings." It's a long list, so I am going to go ahead and number the issues:

1. Dilution from Stock Options, Preferred Shares, and Convertible Debt

We'll start with an easy one, dilution. Even casual investors in the stock market have seen or heard reference to "diluted" EPS, but few investors pause to consider the implications of having to use "diluted" (as opposed to full strength?) earnings. For our purposes, however, it's worth reviewing what others too easily assume. What exactly is dilution, and where does it come from? The most common source is stock options. Companies regularly grant high-ranking employees the opportunity to purchase shares at a set price at a future point in time, one that is generally equal to the price at the time of the grant. These grants are part of compensation and long-term retention packages and often show up in small, young companies that may not have a lot of cash on hand to make payroll. Basically these employees are being paid in shares with the assumption that as the share price rises over time and the options "vest," the employees can cash in their chips. Even in large, mature corporations, stock options can be a significant component of executive compensation.

In theory, there is nothing wrong with the granting of stock options, other than the fact that it distorts management incentives to "get the stock up" in time for option vesting, rather than focusing on making the right long-term business decisions. But setting aside that quibble, the existence of options has one practical consequence: it leads to companies printing two sets of EPS figures, one based on actual shares outstanding and one based on the shares outstanding taking into account the option grants. The latter figure is typically lower than the former for any company that has options outstanding, which means that the claim on company profits by current, "real" shareholders is being diluted by the shares that will be distributed in the future via options.

But it gets even more complicated. Companies whose share prices have risen will have more of their options "in the money" (market price above the option's "strike" price) and therefore have greater dilution. Share prices that have declined or just remained flat over time will have fewer options that are in the money. Therefore the dilution is less. The point is that the degree of dilution to existing company owners will vary not only with the number of stock options granted but also with the share price itself. So in addition to having to determine the amount of earnings that might be available for distribution as dividends, investors also have to figure out how many claimants there might be based on the stock options granted and the share price.

As a practical matter, dilution is most significant in the small company and tech start-up world, and even among the larger, more mature companies that can and do pay dividends, the issue of dilution is nowhere near the problem it was a decade ago, when compensating employees through rising share prices seemed like a great idea. At that time, the market had been gaining steadily for nearly two decades. More than 10 years of flat stock market returns since, however, have poured cold water on the idea and have led many companies to discontinue or scale back their stock option programs. (A change in the law that made options granted to employees an "expense" that lowered EPS also contributed to the move away from the practice.) For the S&P 500 Index companies, the median dilution has fallen over the past decade to 1%, but as of the end of 2011, there were still 29 S&P 500 Index companies with dilution over 4% and 10 with dilution over 10%. Notable companies near the top of the list include Accenture Technology (15%), Chesapeake Energy (11.9%), Goldman Sachs Group (8.0%), Procter & Gamble (7.1%), priceline.com (6.3%), Colgate-Palmolive (4.7%), and EMC Corp (4.5%). For the top 500 stocks that trade on the Nasdaq, the median dilution is higher (1.3%): Sirius XM Radio dilutes its shareholders by 73%. Micron Technology is at 18.4%, NetApp at 9.1%, Broadcom at 7.1%, etc.[4] A certain amount of dilution is tolerable and to be expected in an environment when restricted stock or stock options are widely spread throughout the corporate compensation structure. Investors can take that into account as they make their calculations. Dilution can also come from sources other than stock options such as preferred shares, convertible debt, warrants, and the other means by which companies raise capital, and there is nothing wrong with having debt instruments that turn into equity under certain conditions. But as we make our way through the figures used to determine what a company might be worth, it is necessary to keep in mind that not only is the size of the profit pie variable, so too is the number of people who might claim a slice. Remember this when we visit the issue of share buybacks in a later chapter. Then dilution really does matter.

2. Normalized Earnings

Having to deal with just two sets of numbers—basic and diluted earnings—isn't so bad. How about four? Or eight? In addition to dilution, investors have to confront results presented according to GAAP (generally accepted accounting principles) as well as "normalized" or "adjusted" earnings—usually non-GAAP methods of presenting results in a manner that can be specific to each and every company. These adjustments are intended to smooth out some of the volatility associated with accounting rules and to give investors a better sense of the underlying condition of a business. That's all good. Indeed, it is fitting that some accommodation be made for exceptional circumstances when determining the worth of an enterprise. One bad period of operations, a legal settlement, a plant fire, or an unexpected large tax refund need not change the long-term value of a business. In many instances, GAAP accounting properly insists that certain expenses be viewed as "one-time" or "extraordinary" in nature.

This accounting accommodation may have some value, but the widespread use of non-GAAP measures presents a slippery slope that far too many management teams have slid down, to the peril of investors. The reality is that all too often such "one-time" charges find their way into company results just about every year, the dictionary definitions of the word "unusual" be damned. Just recall from your own investing experience the number of times you have heard the media and brokers talk about how a company, before charges and special items, earned such and such.

Given the frequent changes in accounting rules and guidelines (regarding the amortization of goodwill from acquisitions, the expensing of stock options, the measurement of pension obligations, etc.), it would be hard not to keep multiple sets of books. Indeed, to not take certain charges could be a violation of securities law, but company discretion is also involved. In many instances, a company can identify expenses it has incurred during "restructurings" and even call them out to investors, but has the option of simply flowing them through to net income without necessarily printing a second set of numbers. But that would lower reported earnings used for the P/E calculation and therefore the company's putative value. And in a stock-price-driven world, we can't have that!

When taken regularly as they are, these "unusual" charges allow companies to say things are better than they in fact are, all with the blessing of the accounting industry and the investment community, which is so focused on delivering higher earnings and therefore higher valuations when those earnings are pushed through a P/E multiple. Perhaps the most objectionable charge from my perspective is the writing down of goodwill from acquisitions. Goodwill is the amount paid for a company that exceeds the value of the acquired company's net assets. For some companies in the technology space, much of the purchase price may be accounted for on the books of the acquirer as goodwill. For instance, let us say a small but rapidly growing enterprise with $100 million in net assets is acquired by a larger company for $1 billion. So far, so good. The difference between the purchase price and acquired assets ($900 million) goes on the books as goodwill (or as an intangible asset, basically the same thing) of the acquired company. It is viewed as an asset, albeit a "soft one," that will generate profits in the future. But if the acquisition doesn't work out quite as well as planned, and many of them do not, that goodwill will often get written down in a few years to a lesser value, or zero. Wall Street and corporate executives blithely dismiss this as a "noncash" charge against earnings. But while the write-down might be non-cash, it was cash (or shares) that went out the door at the time of the acquisition. If the acquisition was paid for with cash that was sitting on the balance sheet, it was your cash. If it was paid for with shares, you agreed to have your stake in the company be diluted. If it was paid for with debt, you agreed to have your equity bear the burden of that additional obligation. One way or another, your money was used to buy the asset. When the asset or part of it is written off to nil, you are expected just to "turn the other cheek" as if nothing has happened and no money has been wasted. I beg to disagree.

You need look no further than your desktop computer to find a perfect example. In 2007, Microsoft (MSFT) purchased aQuantive, an Internet advertising service, for an eye-popping $6.3 billion. Microsoft paid cash. Five years later, in mid-2012, Microsoft announced that it was writing off $6.2 billion of that amount—essentially the entire purchase price—as the goodwill from the acquisition was now deemed to be "impaired." Microsoft's press release and most of the brokerage community took great pains to note that it was a "noncash" charge. If you were a shareholder of Microsoft at the

time of the acquisition, however, that was your money heading out the door, or shall I say, down the drain. If you became
an owner of Microsoft after the acquisition, the aQuantive
asset was on the balance sheet of Microsoft and was supposedly part of the enterprise that you were purchasing with your
cash. And then it wasn't.

Other charges, typically for "restructuring," can indicate
that a company was overearning in the past, and now the day
of accounting reckoning has come. Yet the higher "normalized" earnings are deemed to be useful for determining the
value of a company, while the "one-time" charges are removed
from the equation. Or as my violin teacher often says of my
playing, it is quite good except for all the bad parts. Imagine
that you run your own business—say, a retail shop—and you
let the front of your building fall into disrepair. Well, when
it comes time to repaint, do you really delude yourself into
believing that the periodic costs of refreshing the storefront
are "unusual" or "one-time" in nature, just to claim that your
"core" profitability is higher? In the real world, businesses cannot get away with such nonsense, at least not for long. And
public company accounting (GAAP) insists that all expenses,
whether extraordinary or not, be acknowledged in reported
net income. However in the never-ending pursuit of better Es
(earnings) that would justify higher share prices, investors turn
a blind eye to the shenanigans of "normalized" results. But my
violin teacher and I know the truth, and you should as well.

The chart in Figure 1.1 captures the number of S&P
500 Index companies each year in the last decade that have
reported "unusual" expenses. Yes, you are reading this correctly. Every year, no less than 60% and up to 80% of all
companies in the S&P 500 Index report such charges.[5] That
means that many individual companies are reporting these
expenses year after year after year.

FIGURE 1.1   Percent of S&P 500 Index companies recording unusual expenses

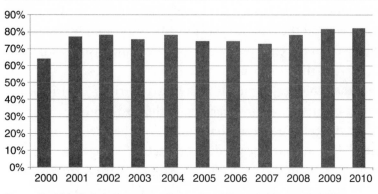

Source: Société Générale Cross Asset Research and Federated Investors, 2012.

And remember what an unusual item represents. It is almost always a loss or expense (though it can in theory be a gain) that means that the company has been overstating profits in previous years by the amount of the charge. (In the rare instance when it is a net gain, the company's profits have been understated by that amount.) In our own analysis of Compustat data from 1990 through 2011, we found two members of the S&P 500 Index have taken charges of one form or another every single year. It's amazing that they have survived as long as they have given those practices. Compared to those sinners, the saints were Genuine Parts (GPC) and Chubb Corp (CB). Both companies have belonged to the S&P 500 Index throughout the measurement period but have had just one year with a net "normalized" EPS result, as determined by Compustat.[6] Let's hear a Bronx cheer for the sinners, which I choose not to identify, and a genuine (pardon the pun) round of applause for the saints. Now to be fair to corporate executives, their hands are tied in many instances.

They may not be able to file their quarterly reports with the SEC (Securities and Exchange Commission) unless their auditors, guided by FASB (Financial Accounting Standards Board) or SEC rules, sign off on their quarterly statements. The rules and personnel behind those rules turn over frequently, such that some of the charge taking ends up being unavoidable and deeply embedded in the "system." That is unfortunate.

At the aggregate level, there's a lot of money at stake. The chart in Figure 1.2 shows S&P 500 Index reported (GAAP) earnings and "operating" earnings (a proxy for "normalized earnings," calculated by Compustat) per share for the 23 years from 2010 back to 1988. Every year operating earnings are higher than the results according to GAAP. Some years the gap is bigger than others, but there is always a gap. The median annual "overage" of profits is 9%. Add up all those charges and they amount to big bucks. According to S&P's data, the S&P 500 Index companies have reported a total of $1.4 trillion in charges and non-operating expenses out of reported profits

FIGURE 1.2   S&P 500 Index operating earnings vs. reported earnings, 1988–2010 (per unit of index)

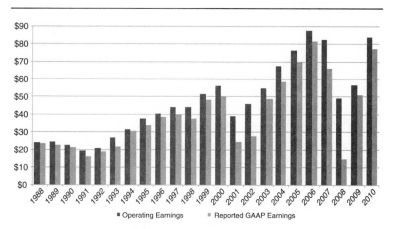

Source: S&P Dow Jones Indices and Federated Investors, 2012.

of $7.7 trillion in the same period. Put another way, operating earnings are 18% higher than the reported results.[7]

Recall why we are looking at this: If we are going to use P/Es to value companies and the market as a whole, we had better have a good handle on the *E* part of the equation. Coming in 18% high strikes me as being a tad off the mark. It's OK in a relative world where one bad number is as useful (useless?) as another bad number, and where everyone is allowed to cheat by about the same amount. But if you are that rare investor seeking to determine the profits that will be available for distribution as dividends, then earnings as they have come to be presented by companies and valued on a daily basis by market participants—this torrent of numbers—are for all intents and purposes of no help.

3. Which Normalized Earnings?

For the time being, however, let's go along with the ruse and value companies based on normalized earnings. Here another problem is encountered. Whether looking for a record of earnings to measure a company relative to its history or for recent EPS to compare it with its peers, some consistent standard is needed. But just determining which "normalized" figure to put into the equation can itself be tricky. Indeed, different data systems offer various ones. For instance, FactSet Research Systems, a large, well-regarded financial data aggregator used by many investment firms, offers a Core EPS figure for each company based on adjustments made by S&P to determine normalized results. The even better known Bloomberg data system reports two separate "special" numbers: the first is Diluted EPS before Extraordinary Items. What is considered "extraordinary" is narrowly defined by the accounting community so it doesn't vary much from regular diluted EPS. But Bloomberg also offers Diluted EPS based on "Normalized

Net Income." When I initially conducted this analysis, the "normalized" result was called Diluted EPS before Abnormal Items. It appears that this figure has had a linguistic "make-over." Is it an example of life imitating art? In Mel Brooks's 1974 comedy *Young Frankenstein*, Marty Feldman's memorable hunchbacked character, Igor, is dispatched to a lab to get the brain of a deceased great scientist to be put into the reanimated creature. Having dropped the jar with that brain, Igor comes back with one that had been labeled "Abnormal." But he just tells Dr. Frankenstein that it is the brain of a woman, Abby Normal. What was Abnormal is now Normalized . . . . And as you'll see in the example below, Bloomberg's notion of normalized EPS is not the exact same as FactSet's S&P Core figure. To confuse matters further, Bloomberg characterizes each year of numbers as either "original" or "restated." And then there are the numbers presented directly by the company itself. These too can change year to year as companies sell off businesses, restate historical results, and offer their own version of normal, one that is separate from both the S&P Core calculation and the Bloomberg version.

In Table 1.1, I have displayed all these figures for the Procter & Gamble Company (PG) for the past two decades. Let me start out by saying P&G is one of the good guys, one of the very best from the perspective of the dividend investor. It's been sending out a check to company owners every year since 1890— over 120 years—and has raised the dividend every year for over a half-century. And P&G is in the business of selling soap. I mean that in a most positive way: the company's products are very popular and its business model is relatively transparent. Moreover, P&G operates in a largely noncyclical part of the economy, and by virtue of selling its goods in just about every country around the globe, the company is somewhat insulated from the business ups and downs of any individual geography.

TABLE 1.1   Procter & Gamble Company Earnings Table

FY ending June 30	1992	1993	1994	1995	1996	1997	1998	1999	2000	2001	2002
FactSet Earnings Figures											
EPS S&P Core (diluted)	—	—	—	—	$0.93	$1.08	$1.15	$1.19	$1.08	$0.81	$1.28
Year over year change						16.4%	6.5%	3.5%	−9.7%	−24.7%	58.0%
EPS (diluted)	$0.61	0.07	$0.73	$0.87	$1.01	$1.14	$1.28	$1.30	$1.24	$1.04	$1.55
Year over year change		N/A	N/A	0.0%	15.5%	13.2%	12.5%	1.2%	−4.6%	−16.2%	49.3%
Bloomberg's Earnings Figures	Original	Original	Original	Original	Original	Original	Original	Original	Original	Original	Original
Normalized EPS (diluted)	$0.66	0.06	$0.77	$0.93	$1.07	$1.14	$1.28	$1.43	$1.48	$1.56	$1.80
Year over year change		N/A	N/A	20.1%	15.4%	6.5%	12.3%	11.3%	3.5%	5.8%	15.1%
Diluted EPS Before XO Items	$0.66	0.06	$0.77	$0.93	$1.07	$1.14	$1.28	$1.30	$1.24	$1.04	$1.55
Year over year change		N/A	N/A	20.1%	15.4%	6.5%	12.3%	1.2%	−4.6%	−16.2%	49.3%
Diluted EPS	$0.66	(0.28)	$0.77	$0.93	$1.07	$1.14	$1.28	$1.30	$1.24	$1.04	$1.55
Year over year change		N/A	N/A	20.1%	15.4%	6.5%	12.3%	1.2%	−4.6%	−16.2%	49.3%
Procter & Gamble Earnings Figures											
Diluted EPS— annual report	0.61	(0.24)	0.73	$0.87	$1.01	$1.14	$1.28	$1.30	$1.24	$1.04	$1.55
Year over year change		N/A	N/A	19.6%	16.1%	12.9%	12.3%	1.2%	−4.2%	−16.1%	48.6%
Diluted EPS cont ops.											
Core EPS								$1.43	$1.48	$1.56	$1.80
"Diluted EPS, or Core EPS where available"	$0.61	$0.63	$0.73	$0.93	$1.07	$1.14	$1.28	$1.43	$1.48	$1.56	$1.80
Year over year change		3.3%	15.9%	27.1%	15.4%	6.5%	12.3%	11.3%	3.5%	5.8%	15.1%

Source: FactSet Research Systems, Bloomberg L.P., company reports, and Federated Investors, 2012.
Note: Company data is from most recent annual report available.

2003	2004	2005	2006	2007	2008	2009	2010	2011	2012	Median Growth	Standard Deviation
$1.58	$2.17	$2.45	$2.60	$2.96	$3.24	$3.38	$3.53	$3.95	$3.54		
23.4%	37.3%	12.9%	6.1%	13.8%	9.5%	4.3%	4.4%	11.9%	-10.4%	8.0%	19.0%
$1.85	$2.32	$2.66	$2.64	$3.04	$3.64	$3.58	$3.53	$3.93	$3.12		
19.4%	25.7%	14.7%	-0.8%	15.2%	19.7%	-1.6%	-1.4%	11.3%	-20.6%	11.9%	16.1%
Original	Original	Restated	Original	Original	Restated	Restated	Restated	Original	Original		
$2.04	$2.32	$2.53	$2.64	$3.04	$3.42	$3.47	$3.67	$3.95	$3.85		
13.6%	13.7%	9.1%	4.3%	15.2%	12.5%	1.5%	5.8%	7.6%	-2.5%	10.2%	5.8%
$1.85	$2.32	$2.53	$2.64	$3.04	$3.56	$3.39	$3.53	$3.93	$3.12		
19.4%	25.7%	9.1%	4.3%	15.2%	17.1%	-4.8%	4.1%	11.3%	-20.6%	10.2%	15.9%
$1.85	$2.32	$2.53	$2.64	$3.04	$3.64	$4.26	$4.11	$3.93	$3.66		
19.4%	25.7%	9.1%	4.3%	15.2%	19.7%	17.0%	-3.5%	-4.4%	-6.9%	10.7%	15.1%
$1.85	$2.32	$2.66	$2.64	$3.04	$3.64	$4.26	$4.11	$3.93	$3.66		
19.4%	25.7%	14.7%	-0.8%	15.2%	19.7%	17.0%	-3.5%	-4.4%	-6.9%	13.8%	15.2%
			$2.49	$2.79	$3.36	$3.35	$3.47	$3.85	$3.12		
$2.04			$2.85	$3.15	$3.50	$3.47	$3.61	$3.87	$3.85		
$2.04	**$2.32**	**$2.66**	**$2.85**	**$3.15**	**$3.50**	**$3.47**	**$3.61**	**$3.87**	**$3.85**		
13.6%	13.7%	14.7%	7.1%	10.5%	11.1%	-0.9%	4.0%	7.2%	-0.5%	10.8%	6.6%

Now an earnings table like this might be used by an investment analyst to determine what P/E P&G normally trades at, or used in conjunction with a similar table for other companies. The end goal is the same: relative valuation of a stock, relative to its past or relative to others. Yet, tracking P&G's earnings over the past 20 years is nothing short of chaos. Beyond having regular versus diluted earnings throughout due to stock option and preferred debt dilution, P&G had five years of restructuring starting in the late 1990s that resulted in a non-GAAP "core" EPS figure. In recent years, P&G has sold off several businesses, thus bookending the large acquisitions the company had made earlier in the decade. (Oh, to be an investment banker, collecting a handsome fee at each transaction!) Those sales and a new round of restructuring that was just announced have led to yet another series of "core" EPS results as well as the further complication of reported EPS from continuing operations and EPS from discontinued operations—the businesses to be sold.

Now to be fair to P&G, many of the numbers coming from the various data vendors over the past 20 years agree with one another, but to be even fairer to investors, there are way, way too many of these numbers and they vary too much to expect that tracking any single one of them—even if you could do that reasonably well—would be helpful in understanding the key question for an investor (What is a company worth based on its payments to owners?) and the key question for the speculator (What do other people think it may be worth?). And these are annual numbers. Multiply by four and you get a lot of figures to ponder if you are trying to make an investment decision based on near-term results.

Maybe it would not be such a burden if each earnings variant were consistent in its trajectory. But they are not. Under each row of earnings figures, I've added the percentage growth over the previous year. P&G is to be commended for having had such success in expanding its business over the years, and doing so with laudable consistency, but let's take a closer look at those year-over-year gains. On the far right of the table, I've added a column that shows the standard deviation—the degree to which the results have jumped around—of the growth rates. The answer is a lot, even after adjusting (see how hard it is not to normalize!) for some really sharp up-and-down performance in the early 1990s. Most of the earnings growth figures have standard deviations in the teens, which is really quite high. One is as low as 5.8%. When I put together a composite earnings record—the last row, in bold—consisting of the company's preferred "core" figure plus the reported diluted earnings per share number from the company in those years when it did not take a charge, the standard deviation is still 6.6%. Let's give P&G a well-deserved break and stick with the numbers that generate only 6% volatility.

4. Earnings Estimates

Think I'm done? Not yet. We need to add yet another series of numbers to the P&G earnings equation. The stock market is supposed to be a discounting mechanism. That is, participants in the market make investment decisions based on what they think something might be worth at some point in the future. Dividend investors look at a company and see, in addition to the current profit distribution, growth in those payments, and come to a conclusion as to whether the business at the current price makes a good investment over a multiyear, if not a multidecade, period. But we are, alas, still a small minority in a vast population of would-be buyers who are focused only 6 or 12 months out and as a result, necessarily, care not a whit about the dividend, just about the movement in the share price. For these individuals *cum* speculators, near-term earnings do matter, as that is all they have to work with. That's where earnings estimates come in. You've probably heard reference to "consensus" estimates, which is the median view of all the brokerages as to what a company might earn in the next quarter or year. (It goes without saying that these estimates are for diluted, normalized earnings.) As a practical matter, these estimates may be more important than what the company actually reports, as the latter tell us only about the past, while the estimates foretell (or are supposed to) the future.

In Table 1.2, I have listed what the brokerage community over the past 20 years has expected P&G to earn in the course of the company's fiscal year, at the start of that period. (P&G has a July 1 through June 30 fiscal year.) In the second row, I have compared it to the company's actual results, and in the third line, in an effort to tilt the scales as much as possible toward legitimizing the earnings game as it is currently played, I have compared both with the "best fit" composite earnings from the matrix above. As you can see, that best fit isn't a very good fit at all. In fact the brokerage community is generally quite a bit off. For the last couple of years, when P&G has sold businesses, the estimates made before those sales have necessarily been well wide of the final mark, but that too is important to note. If the stock market is a discounting mechanism for future profits, the chance of correctly estimating those prof-

TABLE 1.2   Consensus Earnings Estimates for P&G

	1993	1994	1995	1996	1997	1998	1999	2000	2001
Consensus earnings estimates for FY, at beginning of FY	$0.73	$0.80	$0.90	$1.06	$1.21	$1.36	$1.47	$1.60	$1.62
Delta with actual	(0.97)	(0.07)	(0.03)	(0.05)	(0.07)	(0.08)	(0.18)	(0.36)	(0.58)
Delta with actual/core	(0.10)	(0.07)	0.03	(0.06)	(0.07)	(0.08)	(0.04)	(0.13)	(0.06)

Source: Sanford C. Bernstein & Co. and Federated Investors, 2012.

its goes down when there are a lot of asset sales and restated results. Note that in two-thirds of the cases, the consensus estimates at the beginning of the year are too optimistic. The company comes in light. It seems that Wall Street's perennial optimism is too great even for an impressive and steady grower like P&G. (Other studies have shown that Wall Street analyst estimates are on average about 20% too bullish.)

At this point, I can hear you begging for mercy, that I am torturing you with data, and minutiae at that. But the sad reality is that this is how the stock market works and how your retirement nest egg is being managed. If you prefer, you can stash your savings in the mattress. Then you'll know exactly how much you have. But then you get wiped out by inflation, as well as having a lumpy mattress. No, it is better to make the effort to understand how the stock market works rather than to turn a blind eye to it and hope for the best. So one last round of torture, and then I'll set you free. In fact, if you can hold on a little longer, I promise to offer up a soothing balm for the psychic wounds that I have inflicted.

5. "Beat by a Penny"

Heretofore I've been using annual results: the 12-month numbers reported by the company, the yearly numbers gathered by the data aggregators, and the forecasted annual earnings put

2002	2003	2004	2005	2006	2007	2008	2009	2010	2011	2012
$1.66	$1.97	$2.24	$2.56	$2.93	$2.99	$3.48	$3.87	$3.78	$3.99	$4.27
(0.12)	(0.13)	0.08	0.10	(0.29)	0.05	0.16	0.39	0.33	(0.06)	(0.61)
0.14	0.07	0.08	0.10	(0.08)	0.16	0.02	(0.40)	(0.17)	(0.12)	(0.42)

out by the brokerages. But publicly traded companies in this country must report their results quarterly. So the whole exercise—multiple sets of results, estimates, etc.—gets repeated four times each year. Yet there is something peculiar going on here. I noted earlier how estimates at the beginning of the year tend to be high and are most certainly off from what a company—even an easy company to track like P&G—will generate. But when we look at the quarterly results, a different picture emerges. For the decade ending in 2011, P&G has reported diluted quarterly operating results 40 times. In 37 of the 40 quarters, the company met or "beat" consensus estimates. In only three quarters did the company "miss."[8] But wait. Weren't the annual estimates usually too high? How can that be? How can a company come in below the estimate at the annual level but consistently be ahead of the estimate at the quarterly level? There's something fishy going on here. And it is not limited to P&G. You can find this pattern of "beats" across the large-company investment spectrum.

Welcome to the Wall Street quarterly earnings game. It turns out both conditions are true—the brokerages have too optimistic estimates at the beginning of the year, but at the quarterly level, the company meets or beats those same estimates. That's because during the course of the year, the estimates generally come down. That can result from disappointing earnings early on or from the company either explicitly or quietly "guiding down" the brokerage estimates as it gives its presentations to investors. From the outside, it is absurd, but this is how things get done on Wall Street. I am reminded of the delightful scene early in *Casablanca* where Captain Renault is entertaining Victor Laszlo at Rick's café:

Captain Renault: *Emil, please. A bottle of your best champagne, and put it on my bill.*

Victor Laszlo: *Captain, please—*
Captain Renault: *Oh, please, monsieur. It is a little game we play. They put it on the bill. I tear up the bill. It is very convenient.*

This game is being played with your money. You should be outraged. Why aren't you outraged?

As a young analyst for traditional "buy low, sell high, repeat frequently" portfolios, I was always looking for more information and relied upon the quarterly revelations of publicly traded U.S. corporations to make my recommendations. At the time, I bemoaned that most European companies did not report full quarterly operating results. As a portfolio manager, I now regret that U.S. companies offer so much information, and so frequently. The flood of highly orchestrated numbers coming from large corporations (or small ones for that matter) can lead only to poor long-term decision making by investors.

From the perspective of the companies themselves, the situation may be far worse. For these large, usually stable corporations to have to bare all every three months is a tremendous waste of resources. The quarterly calls with investors, the conference presentations, and the road shows all take up management time and energy that could better be spent running the business. Instead, senior managers spend an inordinate amount of their time trying to sell the stock. I see this every day in my capacity as an institutional investor. But it's not just a matter of wasted time. Executives who have worked at both privately held and publicly traded companies have noted that the pressure on the publicly traded ones to perform quarterly and to show immediate results for investment projects gets in the way of making good, long-term business decisions. Such projects can take numerous

quarters if not years to bear fruit, and in a private company setting, they may well be given that luxury. Long-term
strategic planning is a good deal harder for publicly traded
companies, where projects and people are judged in three-
month increments.

6. Earnings Beyond P&G

If this is disturbing from an everyday company with straightforward accounting like P&G, take a look at the earnings
record of a major financial services company or diversified
conglomerate. Parsing the quarterly results of JPMorgan
(JPM), Bank of America (BAC), Citigroup (C), or General
Electric (GE) can be a maddening exercise. From a simple
"how's business?" perspective—a question that can still be
asked and answered in regard to P&G—the leading financial services companies and large conglomerates offer, sorry
to say, very little means of directly addressing that question.
Instead, they put forth adjustment after adjustment, calculation after calculation. Even from smaller financials, the
reporting can be challenging. Consider the following 2011
headline from a midsized bank. (I have removed the name
of the specific institution because it simply does not matter.
It could be from just about any similar financial services
company.)

FINANCIAL COMPANY X

REPORTS 2Q 2011 DILUTED GAAP EPS OF $0.27, DILUTED CASH EPS OF $0.33,

AND DILUTED OPERATING EPS OF $0.26

Board of Directors Declares $0.25 per Share Quarterly Cash Dividend

Footnotes in the press release explain the differences among
the three separate earnings figures that are in the headline,
but the point is that the coda for the EPS array is just one

simple dividend amount. Obviously, an investor needs to understand whether the company can afford its dividend, but it is equally clear that releases like this, issued quarterly, aren't really helpful in answering that question. Or, as the common retort to an embarrassing revelation might go: "too much information."

And it's not just financials. Using P/Es on cyclical companies can easily get out of hand. In a recent popular work on stock valuation, Aswath Damodaran, the leading expert in the field, offered four separate P/E ratios per stock in order to show the challenges of valuing oil companies, whose businesses are naturally quite cyclical. He then took an average and median of the group to see where they stood vis-à-vis one another. There were 16 oil companies in total, so the resulting P/E table is a matrix of 72 entries.[9] Don't get me wrong; Damodaran is excellent on the various ways to value companies, and he is equally clear in emphasizing the importance of intrinsic valuation based on cash flow analysis. He is and should be widely followed by investors seeking the ins and outs of valuation exercises. But in this case, his determined effort to get to a useful P/E ends up highlighting how convoluted such an exercise can become.

Yes, company profits necessarily underpin both "earnings" and dividends, but it is not just a semantic issue when earnings are a matter of the current quarter, are as often as not "managed," and belong primarily to executives to spend as they please, while dividends are a matter of years, are what company owners actually get, and ultimately generate the total return investors purport to care so much about. Estimating long-term dividend growth is far from a fully objective exercise, but it involves much less guesswork than trying to come up with near-term earnings, or a series of earnings figures that are then averaged. As a valuation framework, focusing on long-term dividends is not only theoretically superior, it is also just a lot more straightforward than chasing near-term earnings.

Critics with a longer-term view will charge that I have exchanged one subjective exercise (forecasting earnings) for a different one (forecasting dividends). Is it possible that I am oversimplifying to justify a focus on one long-term factor? Perhaps. And there is still substantial work to be done to assess whether a company has the ability to pay and increase profit distributions to its owners, and whether management has the inclination to do so. However great the challenge of forecasting dividend growth, it pales in comparison to the monumental and ultimately futile task of trying to figure out what someone else might pay for a stock a week or a month or even a year hence based on the P/E game.

Dividends are paid out of earnings, it is true, and over the long term, both must follow a similar trajectory. But the financial services industry, and the businesses themselves, have made such a mess out of earnings—dilution, too many adjustments, too many sets of numbers, and a focus on quarterly results—that they no longer can be used in any meaningful sense by long-term investors. Earnings are supposed to be the means to the end of dividends, but on Wall Street and regrettably on Main Street, the means has become the end. For stock speculators, that's all for the best. But investors

TABLE 1.3   P&G's Dividend Growth for the Past 20 Years

	1992	1993	1994	1995	1996	1997	1998	1999	2000	2001	2002
Annual dividends	$0.26	$0.27	$0.31	$0.35	$0.40	$0.45	$0.51	$0.57	$0.64	$0.70	$0.76
Year over year change		7.3%	12.7%	12.9%	14.3%	12.5%	12.2%	12.9%	12.3%	9.4%	8.6%

Source: FactSet Research Systems, 2012.

who see themselves as company owners should simply focus
on what they actually derive from their stake—the dividend
they receive—and assess the company's ability to support and
increase it over time.

The Dividend

You can relax now. The cavalry has arrived. Table 1.3 shows
P&G's dividends for the past 20 years. They are as reliable as
Tide detergent and as consistent as 99-44/100% pure Ivory
Soap. Note that in contrast to earnings, there is only one
set of numbers, no dilution, no "normalized" dividend, no
"core" dividend. There is no disputing the value of a dividend
when it is paid; it is always a positive value. Regardless of the
data source, the figure is the same. More importantly, note
the growth rate of the dividend over the two-decade period—
an admirable 12% per year. And even more critically, the
standard deviation of that growth rate is very low, just 2%,
one-third the volatility of the earnings results with the lowest
standard deviation.

P&G proudly trumpets the company's long history of dividend payments, starting in the late nineteenth century, and
justifiably notes nearly 60 years of annual increases, since
1954. That's an exceptional record and a testament to a very-
well-run company. If you believe that this impressive rate of

2003	2004	2005	2006	2007	2008	2009	2010	2011	2012	Median Growth	StDev
$0.82	$0.93	$1.03	$1.15	$1.28	$1.45	$1.64	$1.80	$1.97	$2.14		
7.9%	13.7%	10.5%	11.7%	11.3%	13.3%	13.1%	9.9%	9.3%	8.6%	11.9%	2.1%

dividend growth can be sustained, and if you find the current yield attractive, you might want to consider becoming a company owner. The stock market gives you the opportunity to do so with relative ease. A stake in Tide and Ivory, as well as Crest Toothpaste, Olay, Pampers, Bounty, and many other leading brands is just a few keystrokes away.

Yes, yes, you say. That's all fine, but what about the *stock*? Well, here's the point: over time, the share price follows the dividend growth. In P&G's case, since 1962 (as far back as I have detailed data), the dividend has risen by a compound annual growth rate of 9.6%. In the same time period, the share price has gained at a rate of 8.8%.[10] With the exception of the last decade, when share prices have been sluggish, the relationship between P&G's stock and dividend has been remarkably steady: *asset prices follow the trajectory of the profit distributions.* In the next section, I'll produce more examples, but suffice it here to note that over the long term, the relationship for S&P 500 Index–type companies is close, with a high correlation between dividend growth and share price appreciation. So if you like "stocks" (and are perhaps indifferent to the underlying company) and you want them to "go up" over the long term, you should still focus on the dividend.

After all of this buildup and a detailed review of earnings at one of America's best-run companies, let me summarize the point of this chapter: *It's not that you can't play the Wall Street game of guessing near-term earnings in order to figure out where the stock might trade a week or a few months from now; it's more a matter of why would you want to?* That's not how you manage your own business. Why would you treat your investment portfolio—an aggregation of businesses—any differently?

The Stock Market Classes of 1962, 1970, 1980, 1990, and 2000

Stocks go up over time because earnings rise, and dividends are the clearest manifestation of that underlying gain in profits. It's a simple enough concept, even if it is no longer acknowledged on a Wall Street crazed with quarterly earnings and a Main Street that has been cajoled into playing the quarterly earnings game. Stepping back from the example of P&G, there are 154 companies that were trading publicly in the United States on December 31, 1962, and were still trading on December 31, 2010. That's 48 years. Of those, 14 did not have dividends at the starting point, and 13 of them that had dividends at the beginning did not have them at the end. Four companies did not have dividends at either the beginning or the end. That leaves 123 companies trading then and now with dividends at the start and finish.

The scatterplot in Figure 1.3 shows the relationship between the dividend growth and share price appreciation for those companies. The correlation—the fact that the data points fall pretty much in a line—between the two is 86.6%. I would also note that this group had a median total return of 10.66% while the 13 stocks still surviving but with no dividend at the end point had a median return of just half that, 5.33%.[11]

Scatterplots aren't usually found in books on the bestseller list, and that is a pity. The chart provides a straightforward visual representation of an even more straightforward business concept: *the change in the value of a business closely follows changes in the profit distributions of said business.* Statistically oriented readers may object to the overwhelming survivor bias in this analysis. I would say that that is precisely the point: a characteristic of survivors is that they have profits and can distribute them. There will also be instances of com-

FIGURE 1.3   Share prices and dividend growth since 1962

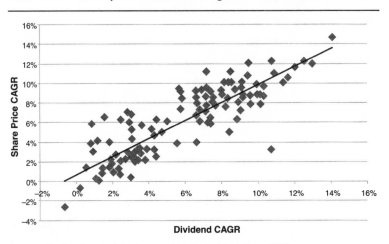

Source: FactSet Research Systems and Federated Investors, 2012.

panies going back and forth on their dividend payments. That will trouble the statisticians, but it should not trouble investors. Investing for dividends is not the outcome of a narrow statistical analysis; it is a basic business proposition.

But let me give you a few individual company examples that make that same point in a commonsense fashion: Abbott Laboratories (ABT) enjoyed annual dividend growth of 13% and share price appreciation of 12.1% over the 48-year period. In a nice instance of pure coincidence, longtime rivals PepsiCo (PEP) and Coca-Cola (KO), though they now have substantially different businesses, came in exactly the same, with dividend growth of 10.9% and share price appreciation of 11.0%. Relatively few companies have identical dividend and share price growth rates. The difference is explained by the yield changing over time. In some instances, investors are now paying more for an income stream, in some instances less. But in most cases, the change in yield is minor compared to the close relationship between the dividend trajectory and the share price path. There are exceptions, such as John Deere & Co (DE), with a 7.2% dividend growth rate and a more robust 9.5% share price gain. (In 2011, Deere raised its dividend 17% and its share price declined by 7%, bringing the share price and dividend metrics closer together.) At the other end of the spectrum, Bank of America (BAC) posted share price growth of 5.9% since 1962, but after its recent cut, dividend growth of just 0.9%. (BAC shares fell 58% in 2011 while the dividend stayed flat. That gap, too, appears to be narrowing.) And then, of course, there are those unfortunates such as Eastman Kodak (EK) that had to discontinue their dividends. Those businesses have struggled, plain and simple, and the results are visible to all. The less said about them, the better.

For the class of 1970 and the subsequent cohorts, I will spare you (reluctantly) the scatterplots and just show the table of results (Table 1.4).

Read it left to right, read it top to bottom. The conclusion is the same: as the market became increasingly detached from dividends during the Great Retreat starting in the 1980s, annual returns declined and volatility (standard deviation) increased. And throughout, initiators and payers do vastly better than dividend eliminators and nonpayers, a group that grows dangerously large—half the continuously trading market by 2000.[12]

For the classes of 1990 and 2000, the impact of declining payout ratios among the dividend payers and the rise of a substantial group of non–dividend payers (often technology companies) can be felt. For those two cohorts, one can say that the close linkage between distributed profits and asset values (dividends and share prices) has been broken, at least for a while. That disconnect continues to this day. Too many investors have gotten used to the notion that the fabulous and justifiable successes of Oracle (ORCL), eBay (EBAY), and Apple (AAPL),

TABLE 1.4 Dividend Growth, Share Price Appreciation, and Total Return through 2010

	Securities			Payers						Initiators				Eliminators/Non-Payers			
Class of	Total Number of Securities Trading Continuously	Median Total Return CAGR		Number of Start/Finish Dividend Payers	% of Total	Correlation between Dividend Growth & Share Price Appreciation for Payers	Median Total Return CAGR of Payers	StDev		Number of Initiators	% of Total	Median Total Return CAGR of Initiators	StDev	Number of Dividend Eliminators/Non-Payers	% of Total	Median Total Return of Dividend Eliminators/Non-Payers	StDev
1962	154	10.2%		123	79.9%	86.6%	10.7%	2.6%		14	9.1%	11.0%	2.8%	17	11.0%	7.0%	4.9%
1970	367	10.6%		251	68.4%	78.6%	11.3%	2.8%		33	9.0%	12.3%	4.4%	83	22.6%	5.0%	6.2%
1980	539	11.0%		339	62.9%	75.8%	12.0%	3.7%		53	9.8%	13.0%	5.1%	147	27.3%	4.4%	7.3%
1990	1220	9.9%		630	51.6%	62.6%	10.9%	4.9%		112	9.2%	14.3%	6.7%	478	39.2%	4.9%	10.9%
2000	2168	5.1%		864	39.9%	49.1%	8.7%	8.6%		226	10.4%	8.2%	12.5%	1078	49.7%	-1.4%	17.1%

Source: FactSet Research Systems and Federated Investors, 2011.

as businesses and as investments, are the norm, not the exception. In an earlier age, all of these companies would be robust dividend payers. (Apple actually did pay a dividend until it got into trouble in the late 1980s; it has just reintroduced a small profit-sharing plan for company owners.)

So let's finish where we started. Why do stocks go up on any given day? Because there are more would-be buyers than would-be sellers. Why? There can be a vast number of reasons, but they basically come down to investors coming to believe that the company is worth more than it was the day before. And why do they think so? Because some news has come out to suggest that the company will do better as a business (earnings) than they previously thought or because the value of those earnings may be worth more to investors (the multiple applied to the earnings). So we're back to earnings, and over the long term, stocks go up hand-in-hand with long-term earnings growth, measured over decades. But in the near term, measured in days, months, and even a few years, earnings simply can't be trusted. Quarterly numbers are too volatile to give a good indication of a company's long-term prospects. And though companies will deny it fiercely, the reality is that quarterly results are subtly manipulated by management to make or beat their "number," the consensus estimate from Wall Street brokerages, which is also "managed" by companies. That leaves us with dividends, the true, indisputable measure of underlying, long-term earnings, and that to which the stock market provides convenient and ready access, even if most investors no longer use it for that purpose.

Conclusion: Share Prices, Dividends, and Total Return

The annual return from ownership of a business is equal to the cash that the business distributes to the owner plus the growth rate of the distribution stream, assuming that the asset value will follow the trajectory of that cash distribution over time. That's rooted in basic finance. I didn't create that math, and I don't make any novel claims other than to point out that the rules are no different if the business happens to be publicly traded, except that the cash distribution is called a dividend and the asset value is known as a stock price. That being the case, the dividend yield and dividend growth will equal 100% of the nominal total return of a stock over time. That assertion makes only one assumption, albeit an important one, about the stock market's "treatment" of a business: that the yield (distribution/asset price) doesn't change materially between the measurement starting and ending points. When that condition holds, the math adds up, and 100% of the investment return can be linked directly to the dividend. When the yield falls during the measurement period—the share price outpaces dividend growth—the total return attributed to the dividend will be less than 100%. Alternatively, when the yield increases during the measurement period—the share price doesn't keep up with dividend growth—the total return attributable to the dividend will be greater than 100%. So compression or expansion of the yield does introduce some measure of return not directly reliant upon the dividend. In *The Strategic Dividend Investor*, I referenced that 85% to 90% of S&P 500 Index returns from 1926 through 2010 came from dividends. You might ask, if the math is so simple, why wouldn't it be 100% of the total return? Well, for part of that measurement period, specifically the 1980s and 1990s, share prices moved up well ahead of dividend growth. In fact, share prices shot up. Dividends increased at a more or less normal rate. The capital appreciation in excess of the dividend growth rate in the 1980s and 1990s is what makes up that 10% to 15% of the S&P 500 Index's return not directly linked to cash payments.

The trading crowd didn't like this assertion at all. They pointed out the obvious: that stocks go up and stocks go down all the time without reference to the dividend. Indeed, you can find instances when a company cuts its dividend and the stock rallies on the news. And then there are those securities that have no dividend and seem to enjoy long and prosperous lives. True, true, and true. And for near-term speculators, that's really all one needs to know to justify focusing one's efforts on trading stocks. Investors, however, need to take a longer-term view, and that's where the high correlation between the dividend trajectory and capital appreciation becomes apparent. (And even where investors looking at non–dividend paying stocks for the long term might want to pause and realize that—in the absence of any cash payment from their holding—they are playing a trading game, not making a business investment.)

So having annoyed the traders with the observation that 85% to 90% of the S&P 500 Index's historical total return can be attributed to dividends, let me really irritate them by predicting that during the next several decades, dividend yield and dividend growth will account for at least 100% of actual returns from the main stock market index. The only variable is the S&P 500 Index's yield. If it stays at its current low level of around 2%, dividend yield and dividend growth will account for 100% of the market's future return. If, as is more likely, the market's yield returns to its more normal 4% or so level, then by definition, over 100% of the market's return will be coming from dividends. Stocks will not appreciate as fast as the dividend grows in what will be a reversal of the trend from 1982 through 2000. Whereas in that earlier period, we saw the dividend multiple (price/dividend) expand, in this instance the dividend multiple will contract. The imbalance that was created in the 1980s and 1990s will be reversed, and the market's traditional return profile will be restored. A future analysis of the S&P 500 Index returns from 1926 through 2026 or 2036 or 2046 will show that essentially all of the return from the U.S. market's main index will have been attributed to the dividends paid out and to the growth in those payments. You read it here. I was going to write that you read it here *first*, but that's not true. You read it first in an early chapter of your finance textbook, or perhaps in the first chapter of that book on business or stock valuation on your bookshelf, or you may have seen it in Irving Fisher's seminal *The Nature of Capital and Income* (1906), or in John Burr Williams's *The Theory of Investment Value* (1938). And the same point is implied, if not actually stated in this form, by others such as Benjamin Graham and Aswath Damodaran. You've read it here just most recently: the value of an investment is the present value of the cash you derive from it. The annual total return is the combination of the annual cash generated and the growth trajectory of that cash stream.

Before I am mauled by that aggressive scrum of bloggers, let me unequivocally state that I am well aware that newly public companies in growth mode won't have dividends, and therefore attributing their near-term returns to the presence or absence of a dividend isn't a very useful exercise, that stocks trade 250 days each year and can move up or down dramatically in that period with no regard for the dividend, and that even dividend-paying and dividend-growing companies can see a divergence between their share prices and dividend trajectories for many years at a time. And finally, I readily acknowledge that a many-year period when dividends are not relevant, such as the nearly two-decade run from 1982 through 2000, is long enough to have a career as a trader and a successful speculator. No doubt. That's not the issue. It's not that you can't make a lot of money trading stocks when the environment is conducive to that type of activity; it's that if you wish to put resources into the stock market and treat it as a business investment, you are going to take a different approach than that of the trader. And if you are looking at the S&P 500 Index as the main part of the market, it should be all about the cash payments you receive. That shift from stock to dividend, from the roller-coaster ride of daily price changes to the more stable income stream, allows genuine investors to make long-term and hopefully wise business decisions.

2

Share Repurchases

Rather than manifest their company's increasing profits by upping their dividends (and therefore allowing shareholders to benefit from a naturally increasing share price), large publicly traded U.S. corporations over the past 20 years have increasingly redirected their excess cash elsewhere, into share repurchase programs. Shifting from "stocks go up because dividends go up" in the first chapter to tackling the matter of share repurchases in this one is far from an abrupt change of topic, though it might seem so at first glance. Indeed, the same widespread culture of speculation that encourages investors to focus on near-term earnings also underpins the same inclination on the part of corporate management teams. Their speculation takes the form of share repurchases. But that is the conclusion. Let us start at the beginning. In this chapter, I will lay out the nominal allure of share buyback programs and try to see them as a businessperson might. From that perspective, they are a very poor use of company cash. Speculators and day traders will disagree strongly with the assertions made in this chapter. And they should, as their livelihoods depend in part on activities like share repurchase programs. Some will find this chapter overtly polemical, but in an investment climate dominated by brokerages and hedge funds—in *The Strategic Dividend Investor*, I characterized it as one big casino—one often has to shout in order to be heard over the din of the slot machines and the whirl of the roulette wheels.

Where's the Cash?

The large, generally mature companies that constitute the S&P 500 Index, which in turn represent about three-quarters of the dollar value of the U.S. stock market, are usually profitable. They would not have gotten to where they are now were they not consistently able to take in more than they spend. Where do those profits go? Investors are familiar with one use, dividends, but alas, not very much (less than a third) of book profits (net income) are currently being returned to company owners as dividends. Where does the rest go?

To answer that question, we have to take a brief accounting detour. That is because the dividend is paid out of actual cash on hand, not just nominal profits that are subject to all sorts of accounting treatments. Those accounting rules mean that there can be a substantial difference between nominal profits and cash actually available for distribution. There's nothing wrong with that, but it does require following the cash around the company's accounts before we can appreciate where its book profits are heading. Any businessperson stuck with a big inventory that won't move or the need to put a new roof on the plant will know exactly what I mean. While the dividend payout ratio based on nominal profits is a handy measure, it does not fully capture how much cash is really in the cash register and can be sent out as a profit-sharing check to company owners.

One big claim on that cash is capital expenditures (capex), the big-ticket items like plant, property, and equipment. (In

the information age, computers and software also fall into this category.) Capex is partially charged against profits on the income statement in the form of depreciation spread over a number of years, but companies expanding their operations at a good clip will have much higher cash capex outflows than non-cash depreciation charges. That is, for those companies, there may be less cash available for distribution than the income statement would suggest. Similarly, companies in a steady state or in decline may have depreciation expenses well ahead of capex and therefore more cash on the books than the profit and loss tally would suggest. Working capital—accounts payable, accounts receivable, and inventory—works exactly the same way. It can increase or decrease cash available for distribution. The same is true if a company has to top off the pension fund in any given year, or might be receiving a tax refund due to a settlement with the IRS over some issue in the distant past. (I aspire to Khan Academy clarity, but if I've fallen short, then I recommend viewing their videos on cash flow and financial statement analysis at www.khanacademy.org/#finance. If that fails, there is always your finance textbook.) For companies where capex is close to the depreciation expense, and where inventory, accounts receivable, and accounts payable are as would be expected, and no other factors come into play, cash available for distribution (free cash flow) should be in line with net income. That is, the basic dividend payout ratio and the free cash flow payout ratio will be the same. Some but not many companies fall into that category.

So we're back to the question, where does the money go? For those few ideal, steady state companies, the question is where do the net profits go? For the vast majority of companies, however, the question is where does the free cash flow go? Let's take a look (see Table 2.1). In 2011, the S&P 500

TABLE 2.1   S&P 500 Index Companies: Where Do the Profits Go?

	2011 Amount ($ millions)	Percent of Net Income	Percent of Free Cash Flow
Net income	$866,845	100.0%	106.4%
Free cash flow (cash from operations-capital expenditures)	$815,071	94.0%	100.0%
Dividends	$264,863	30.6%	32.5%
Acquisitions	$213,223	24.6%	26.2%
Net share repurchases	$358,587	41.4%	44.0%
Sum of major cash usage		96.5%	102.7%

Source: FactSet Research Systems and Federated Investors, 2012.

Note: The change in debt levels and change in cash levels would account for the remaining differentials from net income and free cash flow.

Index companies had an aggregate net income of $867 billion. The same companies generated free cash flow (cash flow from operations minus capex, taking into account the issues above) of $815 billion.[1] During the course of the year, they paid out $265 billion in dividends. That's just 31% of net income and 32% of free cash flow. Only a relatively modest share of company profits is being distributed to company owners. At first glance, that is odd. These are large, generally mature companies growing at some variant of GDP, not small companies growing by leaps and bounds that would need all their cash for reinvestment back into the business.

Such behemoths should be in a position to have a meaningful profit distribution plan for company owners. Why don't they? Well, just over 26% of free cash flow ($213 bil-

lion) was used to buy other companies. (Acquisitions, particularly large ones, generally fail to justify their cost for the acquirer, but that is a story for another day.) All of the remaining free cash flow, some $359 billion or 44%, was spent in the stock market on share repurchase programs. That may well have been the single largest (mis)use of any asset in this country in that year. Wouldn't you rather have had the cash yourself? Your dividend payment, your received share of the profits, your cash distribution, your check in the mail—whatever you want to call it—could have more than doubled had it been sent to you rather than to Wall Street.

The Rise of the Repurchase Program

Your money has not always been wasted in this manner. Its redirection to the stock market emerged over several decades. In Figure 2.1, you can see how share repurchases gradually took over from dividends in what I call the Great Retreat.

The shift from one to the other was facilitated by a change in securities law in 1982—the introduction of Rule 10b-18—that allowed companies to purchase their stock on the open market without threat of being charged with manipulation as long as they followed certain rules. Prior to that change, open market purchases had been less frequent and less significant in scope. In the years after that change, share repurchase programs took off. The lines crossed in the late 1990s, with share repurchases ahead of dividend payments in all but 2 of the past 15 years. From 1990 through 2011, S&P 500 Index companies paid out $3.2 trillion in dividends, but they spent 33% more, $4.25 trillion, on share repurchases. If you look only at net repurchases, which take into account the simultaneous issuance of new shares, the lines did not cross as long ago, but the trend is the same. And the amount spent on net

FIGURE 2.1   S&P 500 Index company dividends and share repurchases ($ billions)

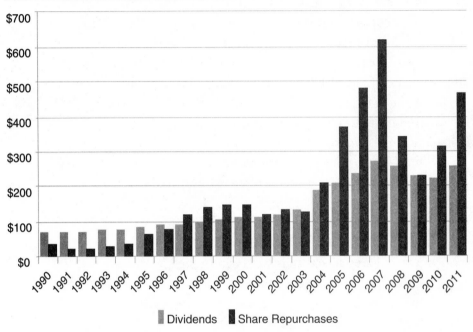

Dividends   Share Repurchases

Source: Credit-Suisse Quantitative Strategy and Federated Investors, 2012.

repurchases, some $2.0 trillion since 1990, is still a material sum. Now to be fair, dividend payments have moved up as well in absolute terms, but as a percentage of net income—the traditional payout ratio—they have been moving down steadily since the mid 1980s, from roughly the 50% mark to 30% currently, just as the percentage of profits redirected to share repurchases has ticked up.

It would be inappropriate to lay the entire blame on Washington for creating the legal framework that allowed share repurchases to flourish. The early 1980s also represented the high-water mark for interest rates in this country. They've been coming down for the past three decades. As I'll discuss later, low interest rates can create an economic incentive to engage in share repurchases. Regardless of the specific legal catalyst (the change in the law in 1982) or the facilitating conditions (declining interest rates), the outcome for investors has been the same: a much smaller check in the mail than could have been the case. Let's address whether that's been a good development.

The Pros

Given the multi-decade-long movement toward share repurchases and away from dividend payments, it is obvious that our view—that company profits not reinvested in the business should be distributed first and foremost to company owners—is not widely held. Corporate America clearly prefers share repurchases to dividends. That's at odds with all but the most recent market history, most mature foreign markets, and even financial theory, at least as it applies to the large corporations that populate the S&P 500 Index. Why is this the case? Why would a large, publicly traded enterprise choose to buy back its own shares on a public exchange? First, share repurchase programs purport to increase the price of the shares in question. More buyers than sellers, and the price goes up. So if a company is in the market buying its own shares, its management team can argue that they are helping investors by increasing the value of their stake.

Point two in favor of repurchasing shares is that the effort can and does increase EPS by reducing the number of shares outstanding. EPS is a simple fraction. It follows that if you reduce the denominator, the value of the overall fraction rises. (Oh, and by the way, many senior executives are paid on EPS growth; buying back company shares can help them get that much closer to a full payday, independent of whether the business is really growing.) Push the higher EPS through another fraction, the P/E ratio, and voilà, you have a higher share price. Let's walk through this math with the always helpful Acme Widget Company. The company regularly sells $1,000 of widgets per year and has a net income margin of 10%, that is, annual net income of $100. Consistent with the current American standard, it pays out only 30%, or $30 per year, as a dividend. For the sake of argument, let's have capital expenditures equal depreciation, and put aside all the other complicating factors (working capital, tax differentials, pension top-offs, etc.). With such a low dividend payout ratio and no pressing needs for capital elsewhere in the business, cash is going to build up quickly. After two years the company would have $140 (2 × $70) in undistributed, unreinvested earnings sitting in the bank.

That's where a share repurchase program might enter the equation. Let's say the ownership of the company is divided into 20 equal parts, or shares. Each has a claim on the earnings, which translates the $100 of net income into $5 per share. We don't know what the market would pay for Acme's shares, but if we apply a not atypical 12 P/E ratio, the price for each share would be $60. The board of Acme Widget then announces a $120 share repurchase program. Were the program instituted fully and at that price (very big ifs), Acme could purchase and cancel 2 of its 20 shares outstanding, a 10% reduction of its share capital. With only 18 shares remaining, the same profits would be divided among fewer company owners, and EPS would rise accordingly, by 11% to $5.55 per share ($100/18 = $5.55). Using the same P/E of 12, the Acme shares might now trade at $66.66 (12 × $5.55).[2]

Without any change in actual operations or the company's intrinsic value, Acme's management can pull out the cigars and claim that they have helped shareholders—not least of all themselves—by getting the stock "up." And in one regard, they may actually be correct. Because the company's equity is now divided among fewer owners, the individual shares should be worth more. Moreover, if a company with an active share repurchase program sticks to its dividend payout ratio, an investor might even see a dividend increase as a result. In Acme Widget's case, the 30% payout ratio applied to the new higher EPS would translate into an 11% higher dividend of $1.67 (30% × $5.55).

So point one is higher share prices, and point two is higher EPS, which should also lead to higher share prices. Point three is taxes. Share repurchase proponents will note that dividends are paid every quarter and create a taxable event for the recipient when they are paid, unless the shares are held in a retirement or other tax-deferred account. In contrast, share repurchase programs don't force a taxable event upon shareholders and instead offer investors the opportunity to time whether and when they sell their shares back to the company and incur, it is hoped, a capital gain. For high-net-worth individuals, this kind of tax planning can be quite meaningful. Moreover, until 2003, capital gains were generally taxed at lower levels than dividend income. Should that situation return in future years, then this tax argument would be heard even more frequently.

Another argument in favor of repurchases is that they provide a liquid market for shareholders who might want to sell their stakes. It's sort of like a return service. You buy the product, and if you don't like it or need to raise some cash, the company will buy it back from you through the market. Companies like to consider their share repurchase amounts, along with their aggregate dividend payments, as "cash returned to shareholders." It's a simple, elegant concept, suggesting that having both dividends and share repurchase programs in place allows shareholders to choose how and when their returns are generated, either quarterly with a check or through a transaction.

Defenders of share repurchases argue as well that the announcement of a buyback program represents evidence of management's confidence about the future. That is, they will claim that senior executives know what's going on in the business and therefore that their willingness to purchase company stock indicates good times and higher share prices ahead. Finally, share repurchase advocates point out that this manner of using excess profits is more flexible than committing to a dividend, and that should business conditions deteriorate, it is easier and less damaging to management credibility to scale back or even suspend a share repurchase program than it is to cut a dividend.

Let's tally up what share repurchase programs dangle before investors: higher share prices, higher EPS (and therefore higher dividends), potentially lower taxes, a return service, management confidence, and capital flexibility. It appears to be a compelling proposition.

The Cons

So what's wrong with this picture? Well, just about everything.

Higher Share Prices

Let's start with the first assertion, that share repurchase programs propel share prices higher. It is true that when there are more buyers than sellers in a market, the price will rise for any given good. And if you add an incremental buyer, how can that not help support the price of a stock? Well, given the number of factors that move share prices around at any given time, it is far from clear that having one more buyer in the mix has much of an impact. But it's more than that. Think through the logic of having a company try to "support" or, worse yet, "push up" its stock price through share repurchases. If the company throws enough money at the market so that it can indeed move the price, it is in effect bidding against itself. Having pushed Acme to $70 per share with its first bid, does it really now want to pay $80 for the second share? What kind of bargain is that? In fact, for that very reason, most companies limit their programs so that they don't "move" the market. So while the explicit goal is to "support" the stock, companies make sure they do not actually affect the price. Indeed, the SEC regulations concerning share repurchase programs are specifically designed to limit the ability of a company to manipulate its stock price: "Rule 10b-18's safe harbor conditions are designed to minimize the market impact of the issuer's repurchases, thereby allowing the market to establish a security's price based on independent market forces without undue influence by the issuer."[3] At that point, as one more of many buyers—and a constrained one at that—the company has limited if any influence on the share price. Perhaps it prevents it from going down further than it otherwise might, but the same logic holds. Why should the company buy shares now if it might buy them later for less? And if the share price is weak, one has to ask, is there another, more fundamental reason why it is declining, and shouldn't the company's management focus on that rather than engaging in artifice?

The Netflix Example

Let me provide an example of a share repurchase plan in action. Take the case of Netflix (NFLX), everyone's favorite movie delivery service. Over the past decade, the company has come out of nowhere to dominate its business niche. The company held its IPO in 2002 at $15 (now $7.50 per share after a two-for-one split in 2004). In 2006, the company raised $101 million in an additional offering of equity, selling 3.5 million shares for $30 per share. At the time, the company claimed the capital would be used for general corporate purposes and possibly for acquisitions. (Curiously, at the time of the equity raising, Netflix had $227 million in cash in the bank. During the course of that year, it generated net income of $49 million and had free cash flow of $62 million. While the company continues to acquire entertainment libraries—accounted for as capital expenditures—the recognized cash cost of these acquisitions has never come close to the amount that Netflix has had in the bank or generated from operations.)

Just one year after raising $100 million with no apparent need, the company announced a $100 million repurchase program in April 2007. By the end of the year, the company had purchased 4.7 million shares at an average cost of $21 per share. That looked like a good trade: buying back for $21 shares that it had issued at $30. The company netted a $31.5 million gain that it used to retire an additional 1.2 million shares: 3.5 million out, 4.7 million bought back in for the same amount. So far, so good.

In 2008, Netflix started on a share-buying spree, spending $200 million to repurchase 7.35 million shares at an average cost of $27 per share. The next year, 2009, brought more of the same: $324 million in repurchases of 7.4 million shares at an average cost of $44. That year the share price rose by 84%, so the repurchases looked smart once again. The following year, the company bought back $210 million in shares, at an average cost of $81. And the share rose a whopping 219% in 2010 so management again looked quite prescient. In 2011, the company continued on its merry way, buying in $200 million of its equity for an average cost of $222 per share during the first three-quarters of the year.

Then business conditions changed, the company announced a new strategy, and it was poorly received. From September to early December 2011, the Netflix shares fell sharply, dropping 68%, from $209 to a low of $66 over a period of six weeks. The bloom was off the rose. In a very different environment, and with off-balance sheet commitments ballooning, Netflix decided it needed capital. In short order, it raised $200 million in equity at a cost of $70 per share. That's about one-third of what the shares had been selling for (and what the company had purchased them for) a few months earlier. Not such a good trade. In less than six months, the company had gone from buying high to selling low. The math was simple: in the first nine months of 2011, Netflix had spent $200 million buying in just 0.9 million shares. In November, it raised $200 million but had to sell 2.9 million shares to do so. The capital loss on those 0.9 million shares bought back earlier in the year was a notable $137 million. To make up that loss, the company had to issue an additional 2 million shares. The company's shareholders would have been much better served had management focused on the business and not the share price.

Despite the debacle in 2011, Netflix's overall record in speculating in its own stock is not too bad: a good trade in 2006–2007, repurchases in 2008–2010 as prices rose, and then a very bad trade in 2011. Did the repurchases help support the gains in the years between the trades? That would be one of the points, wouldn't it? If you compare the overall volume of trading in Netflix to the size of the share repurchase program in 2008–2010, you would see that Netflix did not and could not play a significant role in determining the company's share price. During 2008 and 2009, the repurchase program represented less than 2% of total traded value. That's not entirely insignificant, but it is not enough to "set" the market price for a long period. In 2010, it was just 0.2% of activity. By design, companies do not want to be moving the market price of their shares. Netflix looked good by purchasing its shares as they were rising, but let's not confuse cause and effect. (As of November 2012, NFLX shares were trading around $75 after corporate raider Carl Icahn expressed an interest in the company. Prior to that, they had settled in the $50–$60 range.)

Let me note that throughout this period, when Netflix was generating lots of cash and was buying back its shares, it did not pay a dividend. Rather than send that extra cash to company owners as a profit-sharing check, it poured the money into the stock market. That's silly, but it is not fair to pick on Netflix alone. It stands shoulder to shoulder with many icons of American commerce that have bought back their shares at much higher levels than where they stand now. And no less a stellar group of companies—such as Bank of America—found themselves like Netflix issuing shares at a fraction of the price they had been buying them just a short period earlier.

Though a fair number of academics and brokerage analysts have looked at share repurchases, there is little consensus that they are effective, particularly for the large, liquid types of securities that Main Street dividend investors (as opposed to the Wall Street stock speculators) should own.[4] In our own analysis of the impact of share repurchases on individual share prices, we could find no correlation. Indeed, at the aggregate market level, the timing of share repurchases looks pretty bad, as you can see from Figures 2.2 and 2.3. Figure 2.2 shows share repurchases as a percentage of market value versus the S&P 1500 Index. Figure 2.3 shows the percentage

FIGURE 2.2 Quarterly share repurchases vs. S&P 1500 Index

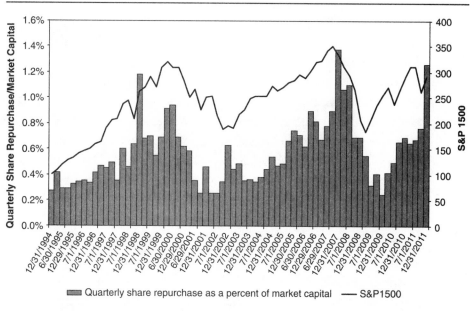

Source: Wolfe Trahan Accounting & Tax Policy Research, using company filings, Bloomberg, Standard & Poor's, and FactSet.

FIGURE 2.3 Company cash flow used for repurchases vs. the S&P 500 Index

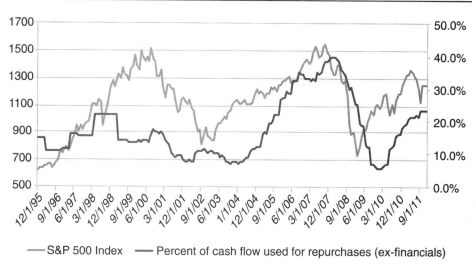

Source: Société Générale Cross Asset Research, citing FactSet and S&P.

of company cash flow used for repurchases versus the main market benchmark.

Both views show the same thing: terrible timing. Share repurchase activity rose as the market did in the late 1990s and mid-2000s. And then when the market went down and share repurchases would have been quite accretive to existing shareholders, the repurchase programs were throttled back. It comes pretty close to buying high and not buying (the equivalent of selling) low. It turns out that company executives are no better at figuring out share prices than the rest of us. I actually take some comfort in that. There is no secret formula to trading the stock market. As market strategist Michael Mauboussin has observed, "M&A and buybacks follow the economic cycle: Activity increases when the stock market is up and decreases when the market is down. *This is the exact opposite pattern you'd expect if management's primary goal is to build value.*"[5] At the individual company level, it's pretty easy to come up with examples of ill-timed purchases, and they are not just from the new economy. According to one analysis, old-economy giant Pfizer destroyed $11.7 billion in value through its share repurchases from 1998 through early 2012.[6] Yes, that's billion with a *b*. It will take Netflix many years to equal that achievement.

There are lots of studies out there that you can reference yourself. If you have access to a public library, I encourage you to do a search of the JStor database for analyses of share repurchase programs. It has all the academic journals that are behind subscription firewalls. From your own desktop, you can search the free Social Science Research Network (http://ssrn.com) for articles on the topic. While share repurchase programs are wildly popular on Wall Street (where they generate revenue for the brokerages, plus underwriting fees for investment banks if the company is raising debt to fund the repurchase) and in corporate America (where getting the stock "up" for option vesting remains a goal), there is just no consensus that they work. And if you coolly and dispassionately look at the reality of share repurchases rather than just the theory, as I've tried to do here, you can see why.

That being said, I am sure there are instances of companies that have been buying back their shares and whose share price levels have been sustained or even increased *as a result* of those repurchases. I just can't think of any. Let me repeat: there are just too many other factors that go into what investors are willing to pay on a daily basis. The great irony is that the academics do seem to have found a correlation between the *announcement* of a share repurchase plan and near- or intermediate-term (relative) stock outperformance. If that is so, it is a victory of short-term stock speculators over long-term investors. Indeed, some smaller-market countries ban open-market share repurchase programs by companies because they consider them to be a form of price manipulation. Occasionally the truth will out. In those smaller markets, that is pretty much the case. In a large market such as the United States, it would be more appropriate to label share repurchase programs a *failed* attempt at price manipulation. The announcement of a big program might push up the price for a while, but then all the other factors that determine share prices come into play.

Higher EPS from Lower Share Count

What about higher EPS? If share repurchase programs end up boosting EPS by reducing how many slices the profit pie is cut into, isn't that a good thing? Yes, it is, and higher EPS should generally lead to higher prices. The key to this working out as planned is that share repurchase plans *have to lead to a material reduction in shares outstanding.* That's the only way it works. If that happens, everyone gets a little more of the company, and the value of those individual stakes rises accordingly. And in fact there is some evidence that declining share counts do correlate with strong stock market performance. So in that sense, the math works out. Let's revisit the Acme Widget Company. It still has 20 shares outstanding, net income of $100 (therefore earnings per share of $5), a share price of $60, and a market capitalization of $1,200. The company announces that it will spend $240 on a share repurchase program to buy in 20% of the company. If the plan were executed on that day at that price, it would indeed reduce the share count from 20 to 16, a 20% reduction. And each of those remaining shares would represent a 6.25% (100%/16) stake in the net assets of the company, an increase of a quarter from the 5% value (100%/20) they had previously. Earnings per share, assuming all other factors are held equal, would rise by that same quarter as the denominator shrinks: $5 per share becomes $6.25 ($100/16) per share. That larger stake in the company, representing a larger amount of earnings, should naturally be worth more.

In the real world, however, this rarely happens. First, while many programs are announced (to great stock-moving fanfare), not all are actually executed. There is no binding commitment by management to complete a program, and in periods of duress, share repurchase programs that were announced when the company was flush with cash can be and regularly are suspended. The second reason is that repurchase programs often do not reduce the denominator as much as the initial announcements claim that they might. Consider the math above. If Acme's share price is rising, the $240 allocated to the repurchase program won't go as far as the planners intended, the denominator won't shrink as much, and EPS won't rise as much as earlier predicted. Let me repeat, share repurchase programs tend to be announced when times are good and the share price is high and/or rising. When the share price is moving up, it's hard if not impossible for the company to buy in the percentage of its capital that was stated at the time of the original news release. But it won't matter, because in a rising share environment, everyone will be happy, thinking management has gotten a good deal and helped support the gain in the share price. Being wrong doesn't seem to matter as much in a bull market. The converse is also true. If a company's share price is declining, a repurchase plan may be able to buy in more of the company than originally intended. That would reduce the share count and help EPS by more than the original calculation. If only management could time their purchases of company stock just so, know when it's going to be up, know when it's going to be down—then they'd be excellent traders. (It's also worth reiterating that higher EPS through share repurchase programs does not mean that the company is actually making more money, it's just being divvied up differently.)

But bad timing is not the main reason share repurchase programs fail to lower share count by as much as originally imagined. The constant issuance of shares is the real culprit. Let's go back to a few of our examples. For the S&P 500 Index companies as a whole in 2011, gross share repurchases amounted to $484 billion, but net repurchases came to the $359 billion that I referenced earlier. The difference, $125 billion, came in the door from the companies issuing shares at the same time that they were buying them on the open market. Some of that amount could have come from actual share offerings to the public, but the vast majority came in the form of shares and options to buy shares granted to employees. It's a two-steps-forward-one-step-back type of environment rather than the grand leap forward companies suppose when they announce large repurchases.

The practice of granting large stock option packages to senior employees isn't as prevalent as it was during the Great Bull Market, but where stock options are still a major component of executive compensation, those executives have an incentive not only to get the stock up for vesting purposes but also to not pay any dividend at all. Think about it. When a company pays a dividend, it sends out a check. Investors know the check is coming and price that into the stock. Once the check is in the mail, the stock adjusts downward by the amount of the dividend. That is, a $20.00 stock that pays a $0.50 dividend will open around $19.50 after the dividend goes out. (This actually happens on the day that the shares trade without the right to the dividend—the "ex-dividend date." The cash payment is made a few weeks later to those holders of record on the day immediately prior to the "ex-date.") Since having shares go down reduces the value of options, those individuals holding large grants generally don't want to see significant dividend payments.

In the case of Netflix, from 2006 through 2011, the company repurchased $1.033 billion of its own shares at various prices. During that period, it raised $447 million, in the form of two specific stock issuances (2006, 2011) as well as option and warrant exercise/employee purchase of shares each year. So the net share buyback was only 57% ($447/$1,033) of the declared dollar amount due to the shares that the company was simultaneously handing out.

How did Netflix's share count fare amidst all this tumult? Before we can answer this, we have to note that in 2006 an early investor exercised previously issued warrants for shares of Netflix that led to the creation of 8.6 million new shares that year. And in late 2011, at the same time that it raised new equity, Netflix also sold $200 million in convertible notes with an effective price upon conversion of $85.80. That is, the company will need to issue another 2.33 million shares (200/85.80) at some point in the future, as long as the share price is above the conversion price. For our calculations, however, that event has not yet happened. But the warrants exercised in 2006 did lead to the issuance of shares that year and are included in our calculation. Add it all up, and from 2006 through 2011, Netflix cancelled 22.95 million shares. In that same period, Netflix issued—directly to the public or to employees or through the exercise of options or previously sold warrants—23.65 million shares. Net change over the five-year period: an increase of 700,000 shares. So all of that share repurchase activity did not lower the company's share count at all, as Netflix was busy issuing shares through a variety of means at the same time and in nearly the same amount. Quibblers will say that I shouldn't count the 2006 exercise of the warrants, a substantial 8.6 million shares. I answer that the issuance led to notable dilution of shareholders through a jump in the share count that year. When the point of the repurchase exercise is to lower share count and raise EPS, then issuance of shares—no matter what the source—is in opposition to that goal. (And please note that I have not included the 2.33 million shares that the company will likely issue at a future time upon the conversion of the new notes.)

Share repurchase proponents might point out here that if not for the repurchase program, the company's share count would have ballooned by 23 million shares, about one-third of the shares outstanding in 2006. Point well made, and it is true, but then a share repurchase program serves an entirely different purpose: rather than lower share count, push up EPS, and therefore share values, *it is simply a compensation expense.*[7] If that is so, it should be recognized as such and not passed off to investors as some means of benefiting them. Now it is true that many companies do acknowledge that their ongoing repurchase plans primarily serve the purpose of offsetting share grants and option exercise. Even if the repurchase program is ill advised and poorly executed, at least that stance is honest, and it can be taken into account by investors considering what the impact of a share repurchase program might be on the dividend. But those companies that make a lot of noise about share repurchases as an effort to "return cash to shareholders," when in fact it is just a form of creative compensation, are being less forthright.

But let's get back to the more legitimate goal of reducing share count. Despite all the money spent on share repurchase programs in recent years, it doesn't seem to be working. If you take the 454 S&P 500 Index companies at the end of 2011 that were in the index 10 years earlier and look at their share counts, they have not gone down. In fact, they have risen. The median increase for those companies in shares outstanding is 3.9%.[8] That is, you the company owner have had your stake diluted by that amount over the last decade despite the popularity of share repurchase programs. As a consequence of the ongoing share issuance, real (inflation adjusted) long-term dividend growth from the broad market is about 2% per year lower than it otherwise would be were it not for the relentlessly expanding denominator in the equation, which divides the profit pool into ever-smaller individual amounts, even as the overall profit pool grows.[9] In theory, the capital raised from the new shares is put to work generating new profits to be distributed in the future. But as the 2% dilution phenomenon shows, it doesn't necessarily work out that way.

Our own examination of share reduction suggests some correlation between reduced share count and better total return, but it is not a very clear trend. We looked at those companies in the S&P 500 Index that had 10-year or longer records and then grouped the companies by the reduction or growth of their share counts. The "reducers" were placed in three buckets (most to least reduction), and the same process was applied to those companies that had seen their share count rise over a 10-year period. The annual total returns of the respective buckets were then compared to one another. Share "issuers" do the worst, which you would expect, given the math of dilution, but otherwise the results were not conclusive. Once again, our view is that trying to game the system through share repurchases doesn't work. Just send us, the company owners, a check.

Proponents of share repurchases will argue here that were it not for the trillions spent on these programs over the past decade, the share count of American corporations would have ratcheted up sharply, and the dilution of ownership for most investors would have been vastly greater. And so we're back to the issue of intent: share repurchase programs that only barely offset share issuance, if that, are not the same thing as "returning cash to shareholders." Other explanations can also be offered. If a company buys another business and issues shares to pay for the acquisition, the buyer may want to soak up those newly issued shares over the following several years. Issuing shares to purchase another business is not, on the surface, a bad thing. And that might be so, were it not for the fact that all the evidence is to the contrary. During the tech bubble, companies were quick to issue shares to pay for one another: it was the case that an inflated currency was being used to buy an inflated asset. That did not end well. But the point that needs to be made here is that share repurchases are rarely presented to investors as a means of taking off the market shares issued for a major purchase or as a form of executive compensation. They are overwhelmingly offered as "returning cash to shareholders," and that is precisely what they are not. Do not be deluded; you risk having your cut of the company profits misdirected away from you.

Higher EPS from More Debt

There's another way that share repurchase programs can boost EPS and therefore, in theory, individual shareholder value. And it is particularly appropriate in the low-interest-rate environment we find ourselves in. If buying back shares is supposed to be good for share prices, then borrowing money cheaply to buy back more shares should be even better. And in financial theory, it is. Let's revisit Acme Widget, which perseveres despite our repeated onslaughts. Acme once again has $100 in net income, 20 shares outstanding (for an EPS of $5). It pays $1.50 per share as a dividend and has a payout ratio of 30%. The company has no debt on its balance sheet. The share price is still $60 per share, and the company has an overall equity capitalization of $1,200 (20 × $60). As interest rates are low and Acme is a good credit, the board resolves to borrow $240, ostensibly for "general corporate purposes"—that is the usual phrase—but really to buy back its shares. The interest on the debt is a quite modest 5%. Before we can proceed, we need to note that interest on debt is a tax-deductible expense for U.S. corporations, so we have to take into account the company's tax rate. The statutory Federal rate for corporations in this country is 35%, but with lots of loopholes and credits, the practical rate is rather lower. For Acme, we'll go with a 30% tax rate. So $240 in borrowed money costs the company $12 in interest, but due to the tax deductibility, the impact on net income is reduced by $3.60 (30% of $12) to $8.40. Total net income goes to $91.60. Acme goes ahead and buys in 20% of its capital with the $240 that it has borrowed. The share count goes down to 16. Divide the company's new net income ($91.60) by 16, and the company's new EPS becomes $5.725, an increase of 14.5%. The company has not changed at all, but by borrowing money, EPS has benefitted by a decline in the share denominator, only partially offset by a small decrease in the income numerator. Assuming a stable P/E of 12, the new share price is $68.70, also up 14.5%. The business is no different, but everyone feels better about it.

Let's do it again. Acme borrows another $220 to buy in a second slug of shares (or 20% of the now slightly reduced market capitalization). Interest cost goes up $11, and net income comes down by another $7.70 to $83.90. But share count is reduced 20% from 16 to 12.8 shares. (Ignore the fractional shares; I'm just making a point.) EPS rises to $6.55 ($83.9/12.8). The company is no larger or more profitable—in fact, the opposite is true: net income is declining, but earnings per share are up. So presumably would be the share price for those holding onto the stock. Do it once again, and you can see the logic—from a theoretical perspective—of loading up on tax-deductible debt, buying in a lot of shares, and watching EPS skyrocket. The financial engineers call this "balance sheet efficiency." I call it dangerous. There is nothing wrong with debt being part of a company's capital structure. And most large S&P 500 Index companies have stable operations, at least in part recurring revenue streams, and the ability to "handle" a certain amount of debt on the balance sheet. But to borrow money to buy back shares ends up being one of those "too clever by half" ideas. Why? Because now the company has fixed obligations that it did not have before. Should the outlook for widgets deteriorate, the company could face the real risk of not being able to meet its obligations. Is that extra risk really worth the opportunity—misguided as it is— to get the stock "up" through share repurchases? By the way, the ultimate logic of borrowing money to buy in shares to boost EPS would leave heavily indebted companies with a much reduced equity base. That is, if you "rinse and repeat" enough, Acme would be left with just one shareholder and a crushing debt load. According to modern financial theory, that would be fine—even "efficient." In reality, however, it would spell the end of Acme Widget when the next downturn in widget demand occurred.

I'm drawing a picture of extremes, but it is to make a point. And it is a point that is particularly relevant in a low-yielding stock market like the United States. In this environment, borrowing money to buy back shares doesn't make much sense. Despite record low interest rates, for most of corporate America, the cost of borrowing is still greater than the cost of equity (the dividend), even after figuring in the tax deductibility of interest on debt. And that doesn't take into account the greater risk of a "leveraged" (highly debt-laden) balance sheet. A recent commentary in the *New York Times* captured the conundrum nicely: "A board has a duty to run an efficient balance sheet. But directors should focus on managing and investing in the business with a view to paying a sustained stream of future dividends. Only hindsight can confirm whether a share buyback was a good investment decision, the main reason to undertake one. There's a suspicion some managers like to engage in buybacks to elevate their own pay, or at least to massage earnings-per-share numbers and hence, the stock market. Those are not valid justifications. . . . If a company can afford to part with cash, investors should prefer dividends to buybacks."[10]

There is one scenario, however, where a buyback financed with borrowed money can make a little more sense, when done within reason. In those instances when the dividend yield on an investment is high—say 7% or 8%—and the company can borrow money on an after-tax basis at a rate quite a bit below that—perhaps 3% or 4%—and if the company's balance sheet, business model, and stable outlook can handle a little more debt, then indeed, the company can modestly reduce its overall cost of capital by shifting from higher-cost equity to lower-cost debt. But in the current U.S. market, this situation is rarely encountered.

Higher Dividends, Lower Taxes

We have a split decision on the next two reasons offered in favor of share repurchase programs. The first of the two is the notion that if a company can reduce its share count and thereby boost EPS—it should not be forgotten that as a practical matter, this is a very big if—and it sticks to a stated (hopefully) high payout ratio, then the dividend received by the remaining individual shareholders would rise along with the EPS. That would occur even though there would be no actual increase in distributable company profits, just a reduction in the number of shareholders. True. But arguing that share repurchases can lead to higher dividends is equivalent to going way out of your way to get to someplace quite close. If a company has the cash, wouldn't it be just simpler to raise the dividend rather than engage in financial engineering?

As to the second issue of lower taxes, here the proponents of share repurchases have a good point. Dividend payments create a taxable transaction four times a year for most stocks held in the United States. And under past tax rules (to 2003), the rate of taxation on dividend income was higher than the rate for capital gains. In addition, capital gains can in theory be timed so that the gain (if it is a gain) can be deferred to offset a loss elsewhere or just be put off into the future. For high-net-worth individuals with lots of investments and complex finances, this ability to time a gain or a loss can have substantial value. I'm not going to deny that. But let's not overplay that virtue. In search of a tax advantage, investors should not subject themselves to notably lower total returns. Remember the earlier charts that show how poorly timed share repurchase programs are? Elsewhere I've written that dividend-oriented securities do so much better in the marketplace than non-dividend securities (our proxy here for share repurchase–based capital gains) that the tax savings turns out not to be worth the effort of shifting the focus of one's investments. Favoring capital gains over dividends just for tax reasons amounts to being penny-wise and pound-foolish.

Return Service, Management Confidence, Capital Flexibility

Numerous qualitative assertions are frequently heard in favor of share repurchase programs. They can be tough to test empirically but can be subject to some basic logic tests. The first is that the company is offering what I've called a return service. It goes something like this: "If you don't like being a company owner, we'll buy your stake back from you." This convenience factor is often tied to the argument reviewed previously that repurchase programs give the investor the choice between collecting a coupon (the dividend) or selling the shares back to the company (a repurchase program). For privately held companies or for very illiquid public ones (where the daily volume of trades is small compared to the overall value of the enterprise), this "return service" might have some value. But not for the S&P 500 Index companies, which, by definition, are large and liquid. The least traded S&P 500 Index company—the Washington Post Company (WPO)—has an average daily dollar volume of $10.6 million. That's quite some distance from the most liquid company, Apple (AAPL), which has recently traded an astounding $10 billion in value per day. The median dollar volume for the S&P 500 Index companies is $115 million in shares per day, every day.[11] In total, the S&P 500 Index companies trade an average value of $101 billion in value per day, for 250 trading days per year. Consider that the total repurchase amounts for the S&P 500 Index companies in 2011 were $484 billion gross and $359 billion net. That represents less than five days and four days of trading, respectively. The point is that a return service for S&P 500 Index companies is simply not necessary. And as we've seen previously, it can come at a high cost due to management's poor timing of repurchases.

Share repurchase programs are also touted as evidence of management's confidence in the future of the business. Granted. That they are. Senior executives know more about their business and its likely future (at least the near future) than outsiders do. And if they think that conditions are good and that the share price will benefit as a result of increasing profits, then a repurchase program is an excellent opportunity to make a little money for the company by buying in the shares at prices below what they soon will be when outside investors begin to appreciate what company insiders already know. Like so many other elements of share repurchases, however, this notion looks good on paper and rarely works out as planned in reality. It turns out that company insiders tend to be far more confident in their predictions of the future than is warranted. Corporate executives are subject to the same forecasting bias that the rest of us are. Second, even if the corporate executives are correct about the business forecast, they can be dead wrong about the stock market. When the market is going down, even companies with glowing prospects generally go down with it. And vice versa. As shown earlier, share repurchase programs have little impact on prices and are most often ill-timed. That is the opposite of what you would expect from the assertion that a repurchase program shows management's confidence in the future. It's nice to have management optimistic about the business, but they have better ways of showing it than betting company cash—your cash—on the stock market.

The final subjective assertion about share repurchase programs, particularly when compared to dividend payments, is that they provide greater flexibility in managing the company's cash stream, and that a small dividend combined with a share repurchase program is a lot less dangerous than having a big payout should business conditions deteriorate sharply. In that case, the company would have to cut the dividend, which everyone agrees is a bad thing. While the goal of being prudent with company cash is undeniable, using share repurchases to reflect this prudence warrants a closer look. First, consider the S&P 500 Index companies. They are generally large and profitable. This is not the realm of the Acme Widget Company. The median sales figure for the companies in the index in 2011 was $8.2 billion. Just the smallest 50 companies had median sales of $1.6 billion.[12] In the grand scheme of things, these are big companies. Some are growing faster than others, some are more profitable than others, but on the whole, they are large and steady. Many of them have highly recurring streams of revenue. By definition, the utilities, the phone and cable companies, the food, beverage, and household product companies, many of the leading grocery chains, insurance companies, and a good number of large healthcare companies fall into this category. It doesn't mean business doesn't vary; it just means that it doesn't vary much. For these sectors, I would argue a higher dividend payout ratio doesn't represent a great deal of risk. Mature, stable businesses can afford a greater distribution rate.

In contrast, those S&P 500 Index companies that are cyclical in nature—materials companies, consumer discretionary businesses, many industrial manufacturers—where results really can move around year to year, are justified in eschewing a very high payout ratio, even on "normalized," long-term earnings. Managers of those types of companies could argue that if they do have excess cash but don't want to increase the dividend beyond what is sustainable, why not have a share buyback program? Here's why: when those cyclical companies have the most cash, it is because they have been doing well, and the stock market is unlikely to have missed that. The share price will be up. A buyback at that time will be the equivalent of buying high. A few years later, when times have changed, the company will have less cash on hand, and the share price could be much lower. That would have been the time for a buyback.

Let me provide a few examples. Consider Deere & Co. (DE), a venerable American icon. Deere produces great tractors, but their timing of share repurchases is typical for an American corporation: over the past two decades, they've bought when the price is up sharply and cut back on their repurchases when the share has fallen or stagnated. From 1996 through 1998, the company bought back $1.6 billion in shares. Then the share price fell, and the buybacks dried up. It was not until late 2003 that the share price rose above the 1998 levels. From 2005 to 2008, the company went back to the well and bought $5.4 billion in shares. Then the financial crisis hit, and it took three more years until the share price recovered to its 2008 peak level. During that dozen-year period, and with $7 billion spent on share repurchases (just under 80% of the company's market worth in 1996 and 45% of the company's stock value at the end of 2008), the company had reduced its share count by just 17%.

Boeing (BA) makes amazing airplanes—and terrible stock purchases. After buying McDonnell Douglas in 1997 and issuing nearly 300 million shares to pay for it, Boeing bought lots of its own stock ($9.1 billion) in the four years prior to 9/11 and the concomitant recession, and purchased another $11 billion in the five years leading up to the 2008–2009 financial crisis, after which BA's shares fell 70%. Boeing could not have foreseen the tragedy of 9/11, but it can see perfectly well that it operates in a highly cyclical business. In that same overall time period, the company's share count declined by 25%, far less than the 42% of the company market value the $20 billion in purchases nominally represented when the cycle began in 1997. The combination of ill-timed purchases and constant share issuance explains the difference.

Or, for an example that you can watch as it plays out in real time, Apple Inc. (AAPL) announced a share repurchase program (along with a small dividend) in March 2012, when its share price was near $600, having risen almost 50% since the beginning of that year. Now, a year or two or three later, as you read this, you can judge the wisdom of that choice. (Don't forget to check and see whether Apple has had a share split in the interim. That would throw off the calculation.) In fairness to Apple, it should be noted that the company stated that the primary purpose of the $10 billion repurchase program was to offset employee stock issuance. That is an important admission that separates it from most companies engaging in share repurchase programs of such magnitude.

This paradox—that cyclical companies engaging in buybacks (rather than having a too-high dividend) are likely to be in the market at the wrong time—leads to the next question: what to do with the excess cash? May I be so immodest to suggest the judicious use of special dividends for highly cyclical companies? That is, rather than have a regular high dividend that may not be sustainable through a full business cycle or waste money in buybacks, how about using an occasional special dividend to supplement the regular payments? It would be a very businesslike solution: after a good year, many private businesses and partnerships will have an especially large draw to the company owners. For planning purposes for the subsequent year, a more normal level of profit distribution is assumed. This approach to above-plan profits is commonly encountered outside the United States. European and Asian firms will often pay a modest regular dividend and then every few years supplement it with a special dividend as cash builds on the balance sheet. That's real flexibility. No less than an announcement of a share repurchase program, sending out an extra dividend check to company owners also shows confidence in future operations, that the company is able to generate profits and that it doesn't need to sit on a pile of cash for a rainy day.

Summary and Semantics

The appeal of share repurchase programs is largely theoretical. More buyers than sellers, the price goes up. When there are fewer shares outstanding for the same company, the value of each individual stake rises. Investors are supposed to be nominally indifferent as to whether their return is generated by a capital gain (the sale of a share that has risen in price) or a check in the mail (a dividend). Given the modest but definite tax flexibility associated with taking capital gains, any rational investor seeking to maximize return would prefer those capital gains and the share repurchases that supposedly generate them. The theory is great. The only problem is that, like so many other grand theories, it doesn't work in practice. The buybacks don't push up share prices, the efforts are poorly timed, they don't push down share counts nearly as much as they claim (if at all), many investors are far from indifferent to their form of return, and the tax advantage is small compared to the risk of capital loss. As a former academic, I love grand theories. As a former academic who works in business, I am very wary of whiteboard, mathematical explanations of human behavior.

My position as a fund manager means that I frequently find myself in front of a company's management team making clear our strong preference for dividend payments over share repurchase programs. For companies that split their free cash flow or simply prefer share repurchases, we are told that the company has many shareholders with a variety of goals. When I point out that the dividend investor generally holds on to his or her ownership stake for many years, clipping the coupons and watching them rise gradually, and in that context derives no benefit whatsoever from share repurchases, the answer often is that the other investors have nearer-term horizons, say six months. In those cases, they are looking for share repurchases to push up share prices so they can exit the position. Isn't it more accurate, then, to call them *share-sellers*, not shareholders? And why should a major corporation accommodate in its capital allocation policy an investor whose intent is so clearly near-term? Yes, it is true that at any point in time, all shareholders have the same legal rights. But in your own business, would you turn your cash management policies upside down to accommodate a customer or a vendor or a partner who you knew would be gone in six months? Of course not, yet U.S. corporations seem delighted to do so, and in an effort to assist sharesellers, they are willing to redirect cash away from you.

Are share repurchase plans always and everywhere bad? No, they are not. Those programs that consistently and over a multiyear period permanently reduce share count may well be judged a success. Given how hard that is to do— timing the purchases, subtracting the share issuances, not taking on lots of debt to do it—it is not a surprise that it happens very rarely. Similarly, modest share repurchase programs whose explicit purpose is to offset share issuance to employees can be taken into account by investors forecasting dividend growth. These are not problematic. While share repurchase programs clearly don't benefit shareholders, some will still insist that they benefit sharesellers. Yes, at one time or another, we are all sharesellers—to buy a house, finance a college education, or even after we're gone and our kids sell the stock. And it's good to get a good price at that time. But the best determinant of what will be a good price is where the dividend is going. That determines share value. Share repurchase programs do not.

As in the first chapter, so too here the key issue is seeing your investment not as a stock to be manipulated but as a stake in a business and you having a say in where the company's profits go. Part and parcel with the share repurchase issue is the dividend payout issue. It is so low in this country (versus history, other developed markets, and financial theory) that it leads naturally to cash building up in corporate coffers. (Granted, some of that money is "trapped" in overseas accounts and would be subject to a tax payment were it repatriated to the United States.) That large amount of money sitting in the till is then used to justify the share repurchase programs in the first place. The argument offered here is that higher payout ratios would be great for investors, smart for the companies, and healthy for the country. Having to meet a dividend payment helps keep companies honest, a form of honesty corporate America would do well to rediscover.

Let me end this section with a final observation: words matter. They frame how we view things. We see this in political campaigns all the time. The candidate who manages to have his or her proposals popularly viewed as "'pro jobs" has a clear advantage over other candidates whose programs may be much the same but who don't enjoy that label. The same is true in business. If someone says a particular act involves "returning cash to shareholders," most people will accept the notion that whatever is being done fits under that general rubric. As in the former case, so too in the latter: it pays to stop and soberly assess what these words mean. Share repurchase programs pay people to go away, to sell their shares, and to take no further interest in a company. How can that be considered "returning cash to shareholders"? This is another of the injustices done by the financial services industry to the English language, as well as to the long-term investor. Let's characterize a share repurchase program correctly: it is primarily a form of executive compensation, and secondarily a form of (usually unsuccessful) management speculation in its shares. In contrast, a dividend is a dividend is a dividend. It is the same in theory and practice. It is an absolute return, cash on the barrel. There is no negotiation, no "net" dividend, no uncertainty as to the value of the payment. Dividend payments fully deserve the characterization of returning cash to shareholders, and dividend payments are what shareholders and corporate managers should be focusing their attention on.

In an open society, the market for ideas (and ultimately for all goods and services) is efficient in the long term. That is, the better ultimately replaces the worse. But that process can take a while, and there can be detours along the way. Consider the AMC Gremlin, plaid leisure suits, and disco music on the eight-track stereo. They were all detours. At the time (the 1970s), they seemed like improvements over what had gone before. But they were not enduring, and they were ultimately supplanted. In financial practice, it is much the same. There is a fundamental conceptual framework that is basically timeless—DCFs and DDMs (timeless though only given formal names and worked out in great detail in the last century)—and then there are passing fads. Share repurchases are not quite as bad as the dot-com mania from a decade ago, the Nifty Fifty from the 1970s, or leveraged investment trusts from the 1920s, but they are part of an outtake from standard investment practice over the past 200 years, a standard practice rooted in basic business. Having a historical sensibility helps here. Practices do evolve and improve over time, but there are dead ends, pauses, and even reversals. Taking the dividend payout ratio down by almost half, using the money for share repurchases, and calling it "returning cash to shareholders" is one of those dead ends.

3

The U.S. Stock Market: What's Wrong with This Picture?

Investing should be more like watching paint dry or watching grass grow. If you want excitement, take $800 and go to Las Vegas.

Nobel Prize laureate Paul Samuelson

Businesses increase in value over the long term because their distributable profits rise. That is, stocks go up because dividends go up. Share repurchase programs, as an alternative to dividend payments, are a bad idea. Given those assertions, there's something not quite right about the U.S. stock market. Can you see what it is? I've referenced before the low dividend payout ratio (dividend/profits) of the S&P 500 Index companies and the low dividend yield (dividend/price) of an investment in the S&P 500 Index. Now I want to address why those figures are a problem and argue that the S&P 500 Index companies should have at least a 50% payout ratio, rather than the current 30% figure. It's harder to define exactly what the yield of the U.S. market should be, but it is easy to assert that it ought to be a good deal more than the current, miserly

2%. The issue, once again, is how we view the stock market and what we as investors can and should reasonably expect from it as a business investment platform. Those expectations stand in stark contrast to the current casino-like environment of the main part of the U.S. stock market, an environment that necessarily turns investors into gamblers. That's not good for the investors or for the companies whose shares are traded there. A higher dividend payout ratio from the main part of the market would benefit investors and, as I'll argue in Chapter 4, benefit corporate America as well.

What Is the Market?

Let's start by defining what the market is. Heretofore I've been using the S&P 500 Index as a proxy for the overall market. And with good reason. The companies in the index—maintained by Standard & Poor's, a century-old and well-regarded financial information service—represent the largest publicly traded corporations in this country. From a revenue perspective, the S&P 500 Index companies more or less line up with the Fortune 500 ranking of the largest U.S. corporations, as maintained by *Fortune* magazine. Of those on the Fortune list, 465, or 93%, are publicly traded, and these companies had sales in 2010 of $10.25 trillion. That's about the same as the reported sales for the S&P 500 Index companies. While a portion of those sales occurred overseas, the vast majority were generated here in this country. To put it another way, the S&P 500 Index offers a fairly good window into the state of big business in America. If you look beyond the S&P 500 Index for other U.S.-based companies that are available to investors through the stock market, there are literally thousands of them. If you take only those with market values greater than $10 million (but not included in the S&P 500

Index) and listed on the two major U.S. stock exchanges, you come up with 3,450 stocks. Total sales for that group in 2011 came to $3.8 trillion, a substantial figure, but only a modest amount compared to the economic heft of the S&P 500 Index companies. From a stock market perspective, the situation is largely the same. The S&P 500 Index companies have a market capitalization of around $13 trillion. The combined market value of all the smaller publicly traded companies based in the United States is just $4 trillion. Once again, the S&P 500 Index really is the main part of the U.S. stock market.

The one notable exception here is that numerous foreign corporations, many of them quite large, make their shares available to U.S. investors in the form of American Depositary Receipts or Shares (ADRs or ADSs). The market value of these companies—such as Royal Dutch Shell, Unilever, and GlaxoSmithKline, among other everyday recognizable brands—is substantial. Those ADRs that are listed on the primary U.S. exchanges and have a market capitalization of greater than $10 million (the same standard for our U.S. small company universe) number 359 and have a market capitalization of $6.6 trillion and sales of $7.4 trillion. Those foreign companies represent quite a bit more in market value and economic activity than the small U.S. companies but still represent just 72% of the sales and a just half of the market value of the S&P 500 Index companies (Table 3.1).

Where am I going with this? It's simple. The S&P 500 Index represents a very good cross section of large corporate America, but it is not the whole enchilada. Investors who want something other than the main part of the U.S. market have ample opportunity to invest in the stock of thousands of other, smaller companies in the United States, not to mention a lot of foreign companies whose shares trade in this country. (Investments directly in foreign markets, in privately

TABLE 3.1   What Is the Market?

	Number	Market Value ($ trillion)	Annual Sales ($ trillion)
S&P 500 Index companies	500	$13.10	$10.24
Listed smaller U.S. companies (above $10m in market value)	3450	$4.00	$3.80
Listed foreign companies (above $10m in market value)	359	$6.60	$7.40

Source: FactSet Research Systems and Federated Investors, 2012.

held businesses, in real estate, etc., expand the opportunity set even further but are distinct from publicly traded U.S. corporations.) Once we have segmented the stock market in this manner, we can start digging deeper and ask whether the S&P 500 Index's low dividend payout ratio and low dividend yield make sense from an economic perspective.

How Are We Doing?

Financial theory and business reality suggest that a low dividend payout ratio can be justified if a company is growing rapidly and sees significant expansion opportunities ahead. If so, it can and should invest its profits back in the business (perhaps as capital expenditures or additional working capital or even to purchase other businesses that will work well with the existing lineup). So the payout question becomes, what is the reasonable growth rate of the S&P 500 Index companies? History is one guide. If you look at the companies that are currently in the S&P 500 Index, their median annual sales growth over the past decade (2001 through 2011) was 7.4%.[1]

Some of that growth would be from acquisitions, and some from sales abroad, but organic growth from domestic sales wouldn't be too much lower. Even after taking into account the modest inflation we have enjoyed in the past decade, the real growth figure should still be in the low- to mid-single-digit range. That makes sense if you look at gross domestic product, or GDP—the broadest measure of economic activity in this country. Over the past two decades, GDP has grown at a nominal rate of 4.7%, a little more in the 1990s (5.5%), a little less during the past 10 years (4.0%).[2] As you might expect from a bundling of America's leading corporations, the S&P 500 Index companies have done marginally better than that as they have extended their businesses at the expense of others, or are in areas that are expanding more rapidly than the overall economy, or through sales abroad, which are not captured in the GDP figures.

So the answer to our question—how are we doing?—is pretty well. The 7% sales growth from the S&P 500 Index companies is a positive number (sales could be contracting), more than inflation and GDP, but appropriately modest given the real-world constraints on companies that are already leaders in their industries in the largest economy in the world. And from a $10 trillion base, it also acknowledges the difficulty of changing large numbers. At these levels, each incremental percentage point of growth represents $100 billion in new sales. Even in a global economy, getting the cash register to ring by that much more is no easy task. Given those limitations, it would be unrealistic to expect S&P 500 Index companies to post "start-up" expansion rates of 20% or greater for more than short periods of time. Yes, the occasional tech company can record 50% or even higher year-over-year sales growth for many years in a row, but though the index may include some shooting stars like Google, they are the exceptions. Big companies—and that's what the S&P 500 Index consists of—are simply too constrained by economics and mathematics to expand at much more than GDP growth over a long period. Unless you imagine every single person on this planet, not to mention billions of aliens across the galaxy, spending every waking moment on an Apple device buying something from Amazon.com, large companies must necessarily end up having their rate of growth slow to that of the economy in which they operate. Don't let an investment banker or brokerage report convince you otherwise.

In terms of actual profits, the figures are not that much different. Since the S&P 500 Index was created in 1957, earnings have grown at a rate of 6.2%, pretty much in line with nominal GDP in the same period, which came in at 6.3%. You might have expected corporate profit growth to be materially above GDP throughout this period. That is because companies generally should enjoy some economies of scale in their operations. All other things being held equal, 4% sales growth should become 6% profit growth, and so forth. It is also because weaker, slower growing, failed corporations eventually are weeded out of the S&P 500 Index as they are dropped from the list or are acquired. Their places are taken by newer, faster-growing businesses. This constant process of replacement should be reflected in the profits of S&P 500 Index companies growing faster than the U.S. economy as a whole. As I mentioned in an earlier chapter, however, dilution from constant share issuance, accounting for about 2% a year of growth, soaks up most if not all of that operating leverage. And companies in the S&P 500 Index can also come apart, seeing declines in their operations for many years before they finally leave the index. (Sara Lee is a good recent example. Love the pound cake; shame about the company.) The point to be made here is that GDP, sales, and profits for the S&P

500 Index companies have pretty much tracked one another at the mid-single-digit level for the past half century.

Act Your Age!

Why is this important? For the simple reason that the investment attributes of a business ought to reflect its general condition and the likely future trajectory of the enterprise's profitability. From a Maserati, you expect speed, not seating for six. Buy a Dodge Caravan, and you can count on utility, not handling in the corners. Mature businesses are by design and practice cash distributive. New and/or rapidly growing businesses generally are not. Businesses in the middle of that spectrum will be, well, in the middle of that spectrum. This basic business logic extends even to publicly traded companies. There is no reason that the S&P 500 Index companies should be treated differently than any other business in this regard. As that is the case, most of the companies in the index—those that are profitable and enjoying steady if modest profit expansion—should be able to distribute a portion, perhaps a quite large portion, of those profits to company owners. It's not that complex or radical an idea. It comports with financial theory, past practice, and real-world business. Why else would you own a mature, modestly growing enterprise if not to receive a share of the profits as a cash distribution?

Historically, the payout ratio for the largest publicly traded U.S. corporations was consistent with this logic. For many decades, from 1926 (when an important data set begins) through the early 1990s, the corporate payout ratio averaged in the 50% range. Somehow, some way, in a manner that would not be recognized by today's money-hungry CEOs, the leaders of American industry during its period of greatest global success were able to invest in their businesses and still send out handsome profit-sharing checks to company owners. It makes you wonder.

Now it was the case then and remains the case now that even among the S&P 500 Index members, companies growing the fastest should have the lowest payouts and perhaps a few should have zero payouts. Whether new or old, growing or not, companies in trouble might also choose not to pay a dividend or pay a very small one. But generally speaking, the more mature companies should have higher payout ratios. A scatterplot of large companies with reasonable payout policies might look something like this: the higher the growth rate, the lower the payout. And vice versa. (See Figure 3.1.) Markets and companies are inefficient, at least in the near term, so there is always room for exceptions, and I've included a few dots well away from the trend line.

In contrast to that reasonable expectation, Figure 3.2 provides a scatterplot of the current S&P 500 Index companies, using five-year sales growth (a proxy for maturity) versus the current dividend payout ratio.[3] It is a messy visual image of where we have ended up after the Great Retreat. If you tilt

FIGURE 3.1   Growth vs. payout ratio: a reasonable expectation

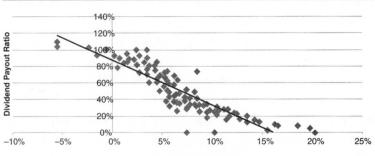

FIGURE 3.2   S&P 500 Index: five-year sales growth vs. dividend payout ratio

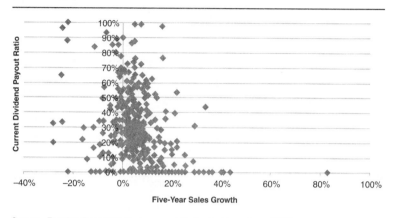

Source: FactSet Research Systems and Federated Investors, 2012.

your head a bit and have some appreciation for modern art, you might be able to conjure up just the slightest curve, to the lower right, but that is a matter of interpretation, not finance. Way too many of these American titans have no payout at all—they are bunched along the bottom axis—and for the remainder there is no obvious relationship between the five-year sales figure and the dividend payout ratio. The overall payout ratio for the S&P 500 Index companies is hovering around 30%, well below what it had been for decades until the 1990s brought a new level of "understanding" to finance.

Critics could argue that, hey, the S&P 500 Index is full of rapidly growing entrepreneurial companies—it isn't, but that is beside the point—that can afford and rightly should have zero payouts. Perhaps, but what about the top 100 companies, the biggest of the big? (The number 100 company in this group had 2011 sales of $23 billion.) These are companies where the mathematics of large numbers suggests structurally lower rates of growth and the expectation of greater dividend payouts. The scatterplot showing the dividend payout ratio and the five-year sales growth figure for those companies can be seen in Figure 3.3.

You might be able to make out, as my seven-year-old did, a bicycle heading down and to the right, but beyond that there isn't much of a discernible pattern. Five-year sales growth is bunched around the 5% mark, as you would expect, but the payout ratios for those companies are in the 10% to 60% range. Those companies with lower rates of sales growth do not have appreciably higher payout ratios. Perhaps the only expected outcome is that the still rapidly expanding companies, those with 20% or better rates of growth, have no or low payouts.[4]

In other words, what is this settled, middle-aged person doing behaving like a rowdy teenager? Nasdaq small caps, emerging markets, commodities, bet-the-company new technology—that's the place to party. The grown-ups need to behave a bit more sensibly. There are bills to pay. No doubt

FIGURE 3.3   Top 100 S&P 500 Index companies: five-year sales growth vs. dividend payout

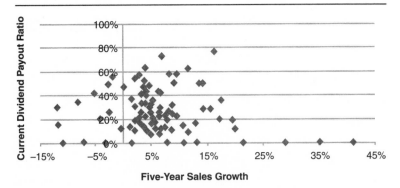

Source: FactSet Research Systems and Federated Investors, 2012.

certain S&P 500 Index companies can justify rocking long into the night, but all of them? I don't think so.

Pays a Proper Dividend: Does, Should, Shouldn't, Can't

The scatterplots make the point, but some individual company examples highlight the imbalance between the state of the business and the level of profit distributions in corporate America. Let's start with some of America's largest and best-known corporations. In Table 3.2, I've taken the top 15 S&P 500 Index companies by 2011 revenue and judged them, quite subjectively, according to their dividend payout ratio. My working assumption is that these businesses, with annual sales in excess of $100 billion, are at the mature end of the spectrum. Therefore, they can reasonably expect sales growth in the GDP+/– range (5% to 6% or so over longer measurement periods) and should have higher rather than lower dividend payout ratios. Those companies with payout ratios appropriate for their growth trajectory are marked as "does." Those that could pay more but do not are marked as "should." Those exceptions to the rule—big but still growing fast—are marked "shouldn't." You will observe that in the $100 billion club there aren't too many of these. And those large corporations that, for whatever reason, cannot support a substantial profit-sharing plan with company owners are listed as "can't." For the sake of argument, I've left one company—discussed in greater detail below—out of the categorization. I've also added—some might say cherry-picked—four additional corporations to make my point.

By my reckoning, 4 of the top 15 are not paying the dividends that they should, and 4 are. Five can't, and perhaps only one of the top 15 can justify not paying a dividend

TABLE 3.2   Dividend Payout Rating for Top S&P 500 Index Companies

Rank	Company	Ticker	2011 Revenue ($ millions)	2011 Dividend Payout Ratio	Rating
1	ExxonMobil Corp.	XOM	433,526	22%	Should
2	Walmart Stores Inc.	WMT	420,016	32%	Should
3	Chevron Corp.	CVX	236,286	23%	Does
4	ConocoPhillips	COP	230,859	29%	Does
5	Berkshire Hathaway Inc. Cl B	BRK.B	143,688	0%	Shouldn't
6	General Electric Co.	GE	141,547	50%	Can't
7	Ford Motor Co.	F	136,264	0%	Can't
8	Bank of America Corp.	BAC	129,913	400%	Can't
9	Hewlett-Packard Co.	HPQ	127,245	12%	Should
10	AT&T Inc.	T	126,723	261%	Does
11	Valero Energy Corp.	VLO	125,095	8%	Can't
12	McKesson Corp.	MCK	112,084	14%	Should
13	Verizon Communications Inc.	VZ	110,875	231%	Does
14	JPMorgan Chase & Co.	JPM	110,838	18%	Can't
15	Apple Inc.	AAPL	108,249	0%	????
17	Int'l. Business Machines Corp.	IBM	106,916	22%	Should
31	Microsoft Corp.	MSFT	69,943	22%	Should
44	Comcast Corp. Cl A	CMCSA	55,842	36%	Should
46	Intel Corp.	INTC	53,999	32%	Does

Source: FactSet Research Systems and Federated Investors, 2012.

even though it has plenty of cash available. Perhaps. Let's go through some of the individual examples. And please note: just because some of the companies called out here have low payouts does not mean that they are somehow not successful enterprises, or that their "stocks" might not go up more than others in any given time period. It is simply to state that as a shareholder, you get little to no cash from a company that is clearly in a position to distribute cash to you. In order to generate a meaningful return from these investments, you have to trade them (buy low, sell high, repeat frequently) successfully. And that, as we know, is speculation, not investment. And it is notably difficult to do over long periods.

ExxonMobil

At first glance, ExxonMobil (XOM), the nation's largest oil company (and number 1 by revenue in the S&P 500 Index), appears to be an exception in that sales growth in recent years has been greater than 20%. But keep in mind, first, that energy prices are volatile and push the sales figure around quite a bit. Second, ExxonMobil has grown through acquisition. The 1999 merger of Exxon and Mobil essentially doubled the size of the company. More recently, the acquisition of XTO in 2010 added a $9 billion annual revenue stream.

The chart of ExxonMobil's sales growth (see Figure 3.4) captures all that up-and-down action. What it doesn't capture is the company's stunningly low payout ratio, 22% in 2011. ExxonMobil prefers to put its money in the stock market, where it has spent an eye-popping $191 billion—yes, billion—on share repurchases in the 10 years through 2011. In contrast, dividends paid in that period came to $75 billion, a significant amount, but a fraction of what they could have been. Has ExxonMobil been a good stock picker? Compared to its two large U.S. peers, Chevron (CVX) and Conoco-

FIGURE 3.4   ExxonMobil annual sales growth

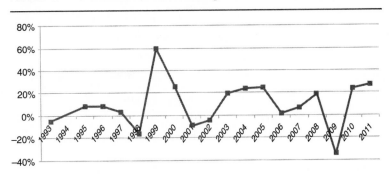

Source: FactSet Research Systems and Federated Investors, 2012.

Phillips (COP), ExxonMobil has lagged. On a total return basis, ExxonMobil posted a 10.41% result (2001 through 2011), compared to 12.73% for Chevron and 12.23% for ConocoPhillips. (Even though Chevron in 2011 had the same payout ratio as ExxonMobil, I would note that both it and ConocoPhillips have more dividend friendly policies than ExxonMobil. Whereas the latter has directed three-fourths of its profits over the past decade to the stock market, the figure for Chevron is closer to one-third: its share repurchases in the last decade have totaled $25 billion, compared to dividends of $44 billion. And Chevron's dividend has grown at an annual rate of 8.8% over that period. ConocoPhillips has spent more on share repurchases than on dividends in the past decade but in recent years has been highlighting its dividends, which have been increased at a compound annual growth rate of 14.2%. That compares to Exxon's more modest 7.6% figure.)

Walmart

Walmart (WMT) is number 2 by sales and an American success story. It has revolutionized an industry and created a profitable colossus along the way. Yet, with $420 billion

FIGURE 3.5   Walmart annual sales growth

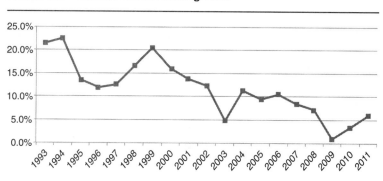

Source: FactSet Research Systems and Federated Investors, 2012.

in sales in 2011, the inevitable slowing is becoming evident (see Figure 3.5). Sales growth has been coming down and approaching GDP levels. There is no other alternative.

Despite that reality, Walmart clings to a miserly payout ratio in the low 30% range. Free cash paid out in the past three years (2009–2011) is somewhat higher at 38%, but at the same time, the company has spent $28 billion—more than twice the amount paid out in dividends—repurchasing its shares.

Berkshire Hathaway

What about Warren Buffett's Berkshire Hathaway (BRK.B)? It ranks fifth in sales of U.S. corporations, with 2011 revenues of $143 billion. Given the scale of those operations, it's not surprising that growth is leveling out at the holding company level, as you can see in Figure 3.6. (The off-the-chart peaks are the result of large acquisitions.)

What does the company run by the United States' best-known investor pay out to company owners? Approximately and precisely nothing. Mr. Buffett can and does claim that he can reinvest the company's profits quite wisely, thank you,

FIGURE 3.6   Berkshire Hathaway annual sales growth

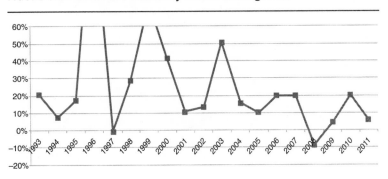

Source: FactSet Research Systems and Federated Investors, 2012.

and therefore that there is no need to pay any of them out. And history suggests that he is correct in that regard. He has managed to "buy low" and on occasion sell high. Because he doesn't pay out dividends, he can use the unreinvested profits from his current businesses to fund future acquisitions. And because he's been pretty successful in growing earnings through his investments, he doesn't need to buy back the company's shares just to boost EPS.

It's good to be Warren Buffett. In that regard, he may be the exception that proves the rule. Unless you believe your company is being run by an investor as shrewd as he is, you should insist on cash payments from the large corporations in your portfolio.

Hewlett-Packard

H-P (HPQ) is number 9 on the list and is the country's largest computer manufacturer. It has grown organically as well as through buying many other vendors, notably Compaq Computer Corporation in 2002. At $127 billion in sales in 2011, however, H-P is slowing down. Organic sales growth has been coming down steadily for two decades (see Figure

FIGURE 3.7   Hewlett-Packard annual sales growth

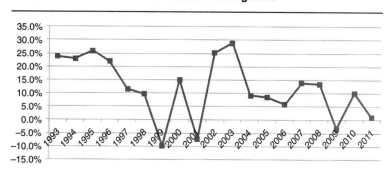

Source: FactSet Research Systems and Federated Investors, 2012.

3.7). The spike 10 years ago was due to the acquisition of Compaq. But looking beyond that period of "noise" in 2002–2003, the trend has been consistently toward moderation in the growth of sales.

In the last several years, H-P has benefited from more large acquisitions (3Com, Palm, and Autonomy, a U.K. software vendor), but the company's sales growth rate continues to move inexorably toward the 5% mark. H-P's CFO, Cathie Lesjak, was recently quoted as saying, "We expect to be a GDP-like growth company with key pockets of higher growth."[5] That's probably a realistic assessment of the company's prospects.

That a company of this size and standing distributes just 12% of its profits as dividends, H-P's current dividend payout ratio, is quite remarkable. On a free cash flow basis, the numbers are even worse. H-P has generated $25.5 billion over the past three years and distributed only $2.4 billion (9.3%) of it. The acquisitions consumed $19 billion, but the biggest use of cash was $26 billion to repurchase its own shares.[6] Perhaps in out-years, those share repurchases will look good, but in light of the company's steadily dropping share price since 2009, they provide a "just so" example of what a waste share repurchases are. As the top technology company on our "should list," H-P might be able to offer up the excuse that it needs to reinvest in its business (or buy other businesses) to keep up with the technological Joneses. That may be, indeed probably is, the case. Innovation is the lifeblood of all companies, no less technology vendors. But in the calculations above, innovation is already accounted for. Spending toward that goal either counts as an immediate expense—in which case it is reflected in the net income figure—or if the technology spending is "capitalized," as it often is, it is reflected in the free cash flow figure, which is after capital expenditures. So in arguing for a higher dividend payout ratio from H-P or any other technology company, the dividend investor is not trying to deprive the company of the resources that it needs to thrive and prosper. It is simply asking that the company's cash—after all its investment needs have been met—be distributed to company owners rather than squandered in the stock market, as appears to have been the case with H-P in recent years.

IBM

How about Big Blue (IBM), number 17 on the list? It is distinctive among American technology giants in that it is not a new company but has been around for over a century. Annual sales growth isn't slowing; it's already slowed, to around 4% annually over the past two decades (see Figure 3.8). That's actually slightly below GDP levels in the same period.

Despite top-line results no better than GDP, in its most recent year IBM paid out only 23% of its profits as dividends. Over the past three years, the company's dividend payments have been modest at best: $9.5 billion out of $48 billion in free cash flow. In comparison, the company has

FIGURE 3.8   IBM annual sales growth

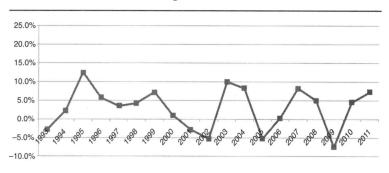

Source: FactSet Research Systems and Federated Investors, 2012.

spent nearly an equal amount, $8.9 billion, on acquisi-
tions—acquired businesses that don't appear to have moved
the sales needle very much. It's still in GDP range. The vast
majority of the company's free cash flow has gone to share
repurchases—a whopping $37.8 billion worth, more than
four times the amount of the dividend.[7] If you are a shareholder, you had better hope that IBM picks stocks as well
as it provides computer services. Because that is how your
portion of the profits is being spent.

Microsoft

As a business, Microsoft (MSFT) (number 31 on the list) is
still posting very impressive growth in sales, but the 1990s
are over. In that decade, the company enjoyed year-over-year
expansion consistently north of 20%. In the last decade, sales
have continued to expand but at a more modest pace (see
Figure 3.9). At the same time, Microsoft has become a quite
stable business, with a high percentage of recurring revenues.
The folks in Redmond, Washington, would resent being
viewed as a utility, but Microsoft's business model is becoming more utility-like.

FIGURE 3.9   Microsoft annual sales growth

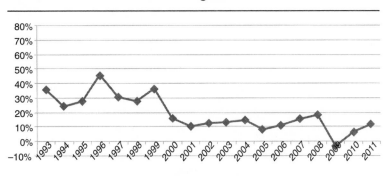

Source: FactSet Research Systems and Federated Investors, 2012.

Microsoft currently has a 30% dividend payout ratio of net income. In the past three years (2009–2011), it has paid out just 23% of free cash flow. At the same time, it has purchased a stunning $32 billion in its own shares. After a "lost decade" (2002–2011) of flat returns—a declining share price offset by modest dividend payments—Microsoft could and should do much better were it to adopt a more shareholder friendly higher payout consistent with its business profile.

Comcast

Comcast (CMCSA) (number 44 on the list) has done very nicely in the cable wars and has emerged as a dominant player, with its own content and a large, national footprint. Over the past two decades, Comcast has expanded significantly, but much of that growth has come through acquisitions. In Figure 3.10, the spikes note an acquisition of a cable company or content, most recently the acquisition of NBC Universal programming. The valleys are more representative of organic growth rates.

Still, let us give credit where credit is due. Rather than pay significant dividends, Comcast has bought scale and heft. The question is, now that it is the nation's largest cable company

FIGURE 3.10   Comcast annual sales growth

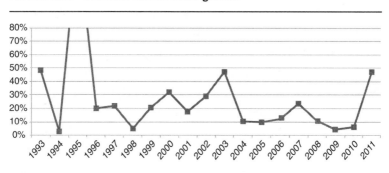

Source: FactSet Research Systems and Federated Investors, 2012.

and has lots of content, what's the payout outlook from here? Comcast is currently distributing 33% of net income and a remarkably low 15% of free cash flow. That leaves a lot of money in the hands of company managers. Will the Roberts family—the controlling shareholders—spend it as wisely as they have in the past?

Those That Can't

To crudely paraphrase Tolstoy's opening lines from *Anna Karenina*, those (happy) companies that are in a position to send out large profit-sharing checks are generally alike, while each of those (unhappy) companies that cannot has a unique set of unfortunate circumstances. General Electric (GE) (number 6 in sales) got caught up in the financial crisis and had to slash its dividend by two-thirds in 2009. Ford Motor Company (F) (number 7) suspended its dividend in 2006 and has only just reintroduced a nominal payment of $0.05 per quarter. Its business is just too volatile to support a high payout. Bank of America (BAC) (number 8) reduced its profit-sharing program to $0.01 per share per quarter in early

2009 as its profits vanished. Valero Energy (VLO) (number 11) is the nation's largest independent oil and gas refiner. Its business jumps around so much that having a high payout would not make much sense. JPMorgan (JPM) (number 14) isn't in as bad a shape as Bank of America. In fact, it is not in bad shape at all. It has emerged from the financial crisis a much stronger entity. But it has also emerged as a more regulated business, and in its infinite wisdom, the government has chosen to limit JPMorgan's payout ratio to around 30% of profits. That leaves investors in JPM stock primarily dependent on share price movements, not cash payments.

Apple

And then there are the "should nots"—those companies whose managers can convincingly make the Warren Buffett argument that they can reinvest profits at a high rate of return and therefore shouldn't pay a material dividend to shareholders. Beyond Berkshire Hathaway itself, the best example may be number 15 on the list of largest publicly traded U.S. corporations by 2011 sales: Apple (AAPL), the current darling of the American stock market. It just reintroduced a dividend, but the payout will be quite small. In recent years, Apple has built up the reputation of a company that makes no mistakes, a company that has its finger on the pulse of the global consumer. Given a string of very successful product launches—I confess to owning an iMac and an iPad, and I have to admit that the latter device is pure genius—Apple can reasonably argue that reinvestment rather than distribution of its profits is in the best long-term interests of shareholders.

But wait. Does Apple really need to reinvest its profits to keep the juggernaut going? Apple is currently sitting on a war chest of $121 billion—yes, billion—in cash and marketable securities, derived entirely from its profitable operations.[8] That amount is equal to $129 per share. The company has that much cash on hand because it has not needed to invest it to come up with the next big thing. So the profits just pile up. What use does the company have for it? It's newly announced dividend is not significant, and a larger but still modest share repurchase program is designed to offset stock and options grants. Apple is really more of an intellectual property and design enterprise than a manufacturer—it outsources a lot of production to third parties—so its capital expenditure requirements are limited. And the company doesn't spend a lot of money buying other businesses. So what exactly is the company going to do with all of those profits? May I be so bold as to suggest that if Apple's board does not want to commit to a "proper" dividend because Apple operates in a cyclical industry and one day may not have the string of hits that it does now, the board should consider paying a special dividend now and again when the cash builds up to very large levels? Microsoft did it a decade ago when it was similarly flush with cash. It is no sign of defeat and carries no stigma of failure for a business to distribute unneeded cash to company owners. Outside the world of publicly traded companies, it happens all the time. In fact, it is the point of the exercise of running a business: to generate profits that can be distributed. Ask any businessperson. In too many ways, the stock market gets in the way of clear and simple thinking about business.

I could continue working my way down the list, but the story would be much the same: large, successful corporations with enough cash on hand (due to low payouts) to play the stock market. To be fair, near the bottom of the S&P 500 Index list, we would encounter many more companies that are growing at higher rates and can possibly justify reinvestment of most of their profits back into the business. There is no denying that. My goal is not to stifle investment; it is to point out that much of the S&P 500 Index is in GDP range and generates plenty of profits and free cash flow, but instead of distributing those profits to company owners, uses them as chips in Las Vegas. Maybe they have misunderstood the observation of Nobel Prize laureate economist Paul Samuelson that opened this chapter and think that their responsibility is to provide excitement and entertainment for company owners. If so, let me speak on behalf of those shareholders to the boards of directors of those corporations: we can entertain ourselves, thank you very much. If we wish to gamble, we can plan our own trip to Las Vegas. And if we wish to gamble in the stock market, we can do that ourselves as well. We do not turn to large corporations for that purpose. We turn to them to make money.

What's the Problem? It Doesn't Add Up!

So the main part of the U.S. market has a very low dividend yield and a very low payout ratio. It wasn't always that way, but it is now and has been that way for over a decade. What, you might ask, is the problem? The problem is that mature companies growing at mid-single-digits with no or very little cash return to company owners makes no sense at all from a business perspective. In private companies, that would not be tolerated. If investors and corporate managers would just step back from their CNBC screens long enough to consider the stock market as they might any normal business, they would realize this. But somehow, just because a business has a publicly traded stock, it is viewed as not subject to the basic tenets of finance. Let's walk through the math. Warning: there are several equations ahead, but they are straightforward. Anyone who has actually run a business will be familiar with them. And those of you faced with making investment decisions—for your own account, for your 401(k)—should have encountered the same issues, even if not exactly in a mathematical form.

The value of any investment is the present value of the cash flows that you receive from it over time—the basic DCF and DDM we reviewed in the first chapter. Not even the dot-commers, the social networkers, or the housing bubblers deny this. If asked, they would (or should) aver that the positive cash flow from their rapid-growth businesses would come at a later stage, and that the present value of those cash flows ultimately distributed to company owners would nevertheless equal or exceed the current prices for said companies. The same logic holds for existing companies that have low or no dividends. They might be able to justify investing everything back into the business so that some glorious day in the future, they will be able to make distributions to company owners that add up to be equal to or greater than the current price. This holds for private and public companies. The rules are the same. New business models (e-commerce a decade ago, social networking now) do not change these rules; they have to operate within them. If you have any doubts on that score, find a grizzled dot-com veteran from a decade ago and ask him or her whether business fundamentals ultimately prevailed, despite assertions to the contrary at the time that "clicks" and "eyeballs" were all that mattered. Or a decade from now, ask the former executives of social networking companies whether cash flow counted for something.

In simplified form, the basic present value calculation from a financial investment has three key factors: the level of cash currently being received, the prospective growth rate of that cash flow, and the riskiness associated with that cash flow. The math is even simpler:

$$PV = \frac{D}{k - g}$$

PV is the present value of the investment, D is the cash that you expect to receive in the next 12 months—the dividend—k is the discount or risk factor, and g is the rate at which you expect the cash flow (D) to grow over time. If you plug in the numbers and get a present value that is equal to or greater than the purchase price of the investment, it's a good thing. If it is less than the purchase price, that's a money-losing proposition. The formula is grossly oversimplified. It assumes constant growth of the cash flow and a single measure of riskiness. In the real world, cash flows are variable, and risk changes along with the maturity level of a business. Still, this formula—known as the Gordon constant growth dividend discount model (DDM)—is useful when trying to understand what it means from a business perspective when we look at the U.S. stock market in aggregate and see a dividend payout ratio that translates into a very low yield, currently around 2%.

The DDM is the sibling of the somewhat more complicated but much more widely applicable NPV (net present value) formula that everyone in the business world should be familiar with. This formula takes into account what a project might cost and the benefits that a business would derive from it in out-years. For instance, if you buy a rental property and need to renovate it, the purchase price and renovation cost would be the up-front cash outflow. The rents received in subsequent years would be the cash inflows. Apply a discount rate to that rental stream to account for the time value of money and the risk of the project, and see what the net present value of the project will be. The same math holds for buying a new piece of equipment, opening a retail outlet, or basically any other discrete business venture. If the project has a positive net present value based on your best estimates and forecasts, it's probably a good idea to proceed. If the project doesn't, you would want to reconsider.

Businesspeople do not knowingly invest in projects with negative NPVs. That's akin to flushing money down the toilet. Yet, stock market investors seem quite willing to accept investment in the stock market where in order to generate at least a break-even NPV, you have to use inputs that defy history, financial theory, and common sense. Let's plug some numbers into the DDM for the broad stock market as represented by the S&P 500 Index. To justify an investment that yields initially only a 2% cash return, as the S&P 500 Index has yielded for more than a decade, you have to have either a very high long-term growth rate or a very low discount rate. Investors typically use around a 9% to 10% discount rate for an investment in the main part of the stock market. Let's be charitable and say 9%. In that case, the math is quite simple. The dividends from the S&P 500 Index companies had better grow at 7% in perpetuity to equal the cost of the investment, that is, the current cost of the market.

$$100\% = \frac{2\%}{9\% - 7\%}$$

If they do, you have justified the cost of the investment, though you won't be making any money in a business sense. If they do not, you are losing money. The present value will be less than the cost of the investment. That's not good. Is a 7% growth rate reasonable for the S&P 500 Index companies? Well, for most of the last century, the market grew earnings and dividends by 5% to 6%. And that was during a period of tremendous American expansion and prosperity. Does the next century look as good as the last one? I hope so, but I'm not willing to bet my retirement savings on that type of math. Moreover, the dividends have to grow 7% not just for the next few decades, but forever. In financial math, it's called a terminal growth rate, and it is a huge red flag to have a value there that is much greater than long-term GDP, which in recent decades has been around 5% or so on a nominal basis. What if we were to plug in the 5% growth rate, keeping the other factors equal?

$$50\% = \frac{2\%}{9\% - 5\%}$$

The present value drops to 50% of the investment cost. That would suggest a price for the S&P 500 Index of just 700, half of its current value of 1,400 as of November 2012. In other words, when the yield is this low, it's hard to view the S&P 500 Index *in aggregate* as investable unless you are extremely optimistic about the future and somewhat blasé about math.

That doesn't mean that there aren't good business investments to be had *within* the market, either individual stocks or baskets of higher yielding businesses. And when you include the foreign and non–S&P 500 Index securities, there really is plenty to choose from to make good investments. But to put money in low- or non-yielding stocks is a quite different exercise: unable to rely on nonexistent or paltry cash flows actually distributed to company owners, investors in these companies have to rely—they have no choice—on the share price changing to make money. If they've got it right, the share price will move up. Buy low, sell high, repeat frequently. There's nothing wrong with that, but it's quite different from investing in a business. In fact, it's the textbook definition of speculation.

The hedge fund crowd and the day traders lost interest in this type of financial math long ago, but those critics who might nevertheless embrace an "invest-as-a-businessperson" approach would want to chime in here and focus on the discount rate. If a lower discount rate were used in our basic equation, then the cash flows wouldn't have to grow as quickly (and unrealistically), and the market takes on a much more reasonable profile. For instance, take the discount rate down to 8%, and the market's dividend need grow only 6% to justify the current price, even with the low starting yield of 2%. That's still not making money, but at least it is not NPV negative.

So is the stock market much less risky than I'm suggesting? According to the formula that has dominated financial theory for the past 50 years or so, yes, my discount rate is too high. I'll spare you the history and details of that theory other than to say that it is based on the notion of a "risk-free rate," the base rate at which, it has been assumed, there is effectively no chance of not getting paid back. That is generally perceived to be the rate on 10-year U.S. Treasury bonds. The thinking is that come hell or high water, the U.S. government is good for its debts, and therefore the rate that the U.S. government pays is the right starting point to calculate risk. Add an additional few percent to the current rate on Treasuries to reflect that stocks are inherently more risky, and you have an appropriate discount rate for that venture. The interest rate on 10-year Treasuries has varied over time and reflects a number of factors, including inflation and expectations of economic growth or contraction. Similarly, the extra risk encountered in holding stocks rather than the risk-free Treasuries, known as the "equity risk premium," can also bounce around. But over time, the formula has produced discount rates for stocks and the stock market in general in that 9% to 10% range. (That coincidentally is also the long-term rate of return on common equities, and it really is no coincidence. The discount rate can also be defined as the rate of return that one might expect to put money into a venture of similar riskiness. As the stock market has returned 9% to 10% per year over very long measurement periods, investors have come to use that as the discounting factor when considering what a future investment in the market might look like.)

At the present time, however, interest rates are exceptionally low, the lowest that they have been since the Great Depression. The 10-year Treasury has a yield around 1.5% to 2.0%. Add the standard equity risk premium of 4% to 5%, and you could get to a discount rate of 6% to 7%. At that discount rate, and assuming S&P 500 Index cash distributions grow at around a 5% rate, the S&P 500 Index suddenly looks reasonably priced, even from a business perspective.

$$100\% = \frac{2\%}{7\% - 5\%}$$

If you are an optimistic sort and feel the next 50 years will be better than the last, and you also expect the "risk-free" rate to remain low, suddenly the market becomes quite attractive.

$$200\% = \frac{2\%}{7\% - 6\%}$$

That would price the S&P 500 Index at a very nice 2,800, twice the November 2012 level. And investors would rejoice.

The question then becomes, is pricing risk off the rate of government bonds the appropriate approach? This is a question not just for investing in the stock market. It affects all business decisions. What is the right price of risk? The reigning financial theory is the reigning financial theory. Until someone comes up with a new overall approach, the one that relies on a "risk-free rate" based on the government's own borrowing costs will be the standard. I can't change that, and I'm not trying to. What I am suggesting, however, is that in a period of artificially low interest rates—the Federal Reserve and the U.S. Treasury have been suppressing rates as part of a plan for economic recovery—using the rate of return on the 10-year Treasury bond isn't a very good way of determining risk.

Or to put it another way, do you—as a businessperson operating outside the confines of the stock market and beyond the reach of pointy-headed academics telling you what risk is—feel that "risk" is at a multidecade low? Are business conditions that good? Is your bank pounding on your door begging you to borrow money from it? Is the economic outlook in your region or industry that strong? Are you that confident in the future? If so, you should be taking on cheap debt hand over fist to purchase new equipment, open up that new operation, hire lots of additional employees, start another distribution channel, etc. As an investor, businessperson, and citizen, I'd like to think that "risk" is at the all-time low suggested by the math, but I rather doubt it. That being the case, the higher (9%–10%) rather than lower discount rate (6%–7%) appears to be appropriate. And if that is so, the NPV of the S&P 500 Index, when it starts with a 2% yield and has realistic long-term dividend growth of around 5%, is—how shall I put it?—unbusinesslike.

The financial theory crowd can make one more argument in favor of very low cash yields from mature companies. And that is that companies have a "yield" that makes them attractive versus other forms of capital, and that when interest rates are as low as they are currently, corporations don't need to have a high payout or high yield in order to attract investors. It's a relative argument—don't give up more than you actually need to get someone's business—in this case, for people to invest in you. So as the "risk-free" rate fell over the past three decades, the need for U.S. corporations to maintain higher payouts and higher yields fell along with it. To make matters more challenging for the investor, this same period saw the rise of tech stocks, IPOs, online trading, and so forth—all of which created for many investors a growing comfort with stocks that had little or no dividends and a culture of trading that didn't involve sticking around long enough to collect the coupon. In this environment, a company with a low payout translating to a 1% or 2% yield could hold a relative attraction—the argument might go—because the rate on Treasuries was steadily declining, and even a paltry dividend payout was of course better than the no-dividend tech stocks. These were relative arguments justifying poor business decisions. Investors seeking excellent returns and corporations trying to offer them would be well served, however, to focus on the same absolute objectives, constraints, and goals with which they run their own businesses. Just because most stock market investors have gotten used to the S&P 500 Index having unbusinesslike terms doesn't make those characteristics any more businesslike.

It Doesn't Add Up: The Case of Japan Tobacco

Let me highlight an example of how a low and "unbusinesslike" approach to profit distribution policies can affect returns. The first company in question is Japan Tobacco (2914-JP), one of the world's largest cigarette companies. Its stable of brands includes Camel and Winston (outside the United States), several popular brands in Europe, as well as the leading Japanese brand, Mild Seven. JT's business is like that of the other global tobacco players: they all operate in a very mature industry with generally declining volumes offset by strong pricing and the occasional acquisition. In JT's case, it acquired the international brands and operations of Reynolds Tobacco (RJR International) in 1999. That's the first spike in sales in Figure 3.11. Eight years later, it bought the Gallaher Group, a leading U.K. and Irish cigarette maker.

FIGURE 3.11   Japan Tobacco annual sales growth

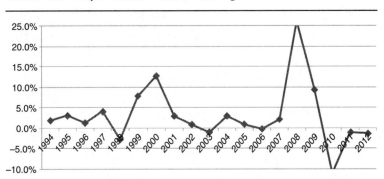

Source: FactSet Research Systems and Federated Investors, 2012.

That's the second spike. Other than these moments, it is low-single-digit sales growth (at best) for Japan Tobacco.

Despite a profile suggesting the ability and the desirability of sending out profits to company owners, JT has steadfastly resisted doing so. In fact, it has maintained an extraordinarily low (for a mature tobacco company) dividend payout ratio of between 20% and 40%. On a free cash flow basis, the payout has varied, but in recent years, it has been in the 20% to 30% range. As a consequence, an investment in JT has yielded only around 1% to 2% in cash as far back as the mid-1990s.

Early in 2012, a U.K. investor challenged the board of JT to materially increase its dividend payout ratio to be more in line with that of the other global tobacco companies, in the 50% to 80% range. The shareholder also sought a large share repurchase program and cancellation of shares held in treasury. JT rebuffed the proposals, calling them "short-term focused," which would constrain future growth and lead to the "loss of business competitiveness and shareholder value." Hiroshi Kimura, the outgoing president and incoming chairman of JT, was quoted in the *Financial Times* as stating that both RJR International and Gallaher had become acquisition targets "because they had to use their cash flow to pay off debts or to satisfy shareholders rather than invest in the business."[9]

As posed by Kimura, those are either/or options. One is either "in favor" of the business or "in favor" of company owners. As I'll argue in the next chapter, that's a false dichotomy. What's in the best long-term interests of the business is of course in the best long-term interests of the people who own the business. How can it be otherwise? Well, in the stock market, it apparently can be. I would argue that the management of JT appears to be confusing what is in *their own* best interests with what is in the best interests of the business and shareholders.

While it is true that the conglomerate that owned RJR International (along with Nabisco and Reynolds domestic cigarette operations) used the proceeds of the sale in 1999 to pay down debt incurred during the famed LBO of RJR Nabisco by corporate raiders over a decade earlier, it is worth emphasizing that the debt was taken on by the corporate raiders, not by the tobacco company. And the sale was part of a series of other transactions that broke up the holding company and led to the relisting of the domestic Reynolds tobacco business as an independent entity. In the case of Gallaher, it is guilty as charged. The company had a high payout ratio and had consistently returned much of its profits to shareholders since being listed in 1997 as an independent tobacco company. In that regard, it was similar to most of its international peers.

Let's look at the returns. Japan Tobacco was privatized in October 1994. Since that time, it has generated an annual total return of 4.32% (through 2011). In Table 3.3, those returns are compared to those of the other tobacco companies for the periods when they traded as independent tobacco com-

TABLE 3.3   Global Tobacco Industry Returns

	Annual Return	Starting Date	Ending Date
Japan Tobacco	4.32%	10/31/94	12/31/11
Altria Group	15.80%		
Japan Tobacco	6.75%	10/31/96	12/31/11
Imperial Tobacco	20.92%		
Japan Tobacco	6.25%	8/31/98	12/31/11
British American Tobacco	24.38%		
Japan Tobacco	3.76%	6/30/99	12/31/11
Reynolds American	22.47%		
Japan Tobacco	8.76%	10/31/94	2/28/07
Altadis	21.76%		
Japan Tobacco	12.86%	5/31/97	11/30/06
Gallaher Group	19.66%		

Source: Bloomberg L.P. and Federated Investors, 2012.[10]

panies alongside JT. (In the case of Gallaher and Altadis, I've used as a stopping point the last month *before* their respective acquisitions were announced or suspected by the market.)

Notice a pattern? Japan Tobacco is the worst performing major tobacco company in each and every measurement period and against each and every peer, by a large margin.

Now I will admit that this example is grossly unfair to JT because throughout the entire period, the Japanese stock market was in a severe and prolonged funk. And despite having a low payout ratio and yield, JT has had and still has a high relative yield in its home market of Japan. That relative advantage has contributed to the company's significant outperformance on a total return basis (dividend yield plus capital appreciation driven by dividend growth) of the broader Japanese market over those two decades. In short, I would have left Japan Tobacco in peace, but it called into question the utility of a mature company in a mature industry in a mature country—and Japan Tobacco fits the bill—paying out a high portion of its profits, and that challenge could not go unanswered. Let me end on a positive note in regard to JT: as a result of the investor pressure, the company did nevertheless resolve to take its payout ratio up to 50% over the next several years. That's a move in the right direction.

It Does Add Up: The Case of Landauer

A large, slow-growing tobacco company with a low payout doesn't make much sense. Some would say that a fast-growing technology company with a big payout also doesn't make sense. And those people would justifiably point to the tremendous successes of Amazon and Google, among others. I do want to point out, however, that a profit-sharing program is not inconsistent with a company driven by technology. Landauer, Inc. (LDR) may not be a household Internet name, but it dominates its industry of radiation monitoring and safety services. Started in the 1950s, Landauer offered stock to the public at the very end of 1987 and started paying a dividend two years later. Since that time, Landauer has paid out a notably high percentage of its profits to company owners, an average of nearly 90%. Yet, despite paying out that much, and in defiance of all the CEOs who insist that they must retain most of the earnings in order to expand their business, Landauer has been able to grow its revenues at a compound annual growth rate of 8.0% over the past several decades. That's pretty good. Landauer's first annual dividend of $0.40 in 1990 (on top of a $0.40 "coming out" special dividend announced at the same time) has become a $2.20 annual payment in 2012, for a dividend growth rate of 8.1%. How did they do that? Given the high payout, Landauer's stock has averaged a dividend yield over the past 20 years of 4.5%. And that gusher of income has contributed notably to Landauer's total return of 15.2% per year since its listing. In the same period, the low yielding S&P 500 Index has returned just 9.4%.

Apples and oranges, apples and oranges. The stock market crowd will object here that it is utterly silly to compare the stock market performance of a small U.S. technology firm with a large Japanese tobacco company, and even that the comparison between Japan Tobacco and the other global cigarette companies overlooks the fact that a great deal of a company's stock market performance has to do with how the country's overall market is doing. Both of these assertions are quite correct. My point is different: however separate in time and space JT and Landauer may be, they are both businesses. And the math of running a business has to add up in Japan as it does here in the United States. The only thing worse than Japan Tobacco making poor capital allocation decisions is for it to criticize its peers for making better ones.

It Does Add Up: The Case of McDonald's

Many large U.S. corporations do "get it." The story of McDonald's (MCD) in the capital markets nicely captures the transition from high growth (no or low payout) to maturity and an increasing distribution of profits to company owners. McDonald's was founded in 1954; it first offered its shares to the public in 1965, and the company started paying a dividend in 1977. Sales growth and the dividend payout ratio for the past 30 years are shown in Figure 3.12.

Despite having $27 billion in sales in 2011, the company continues to show impressive year-over-year gains in revenue.

FIGURE 3.12   McDonald's annual sales growth and dividend payout ratio

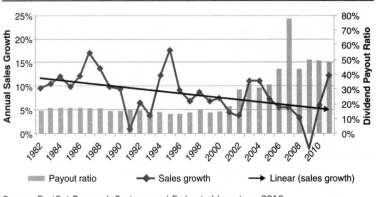

Source: FactSet Research Systems and Federated Investors, 2012.

Still, the sales trend line points squarely at the 5% number. That is its fate.

From 1977, when McDonald's initiated its dividend, through early in the 2000s, the company maintained a payout below 20%. In 2002 and 2003, McDonald's ran into significant operational difficulties in part because it had been opening up too many new locations. In 2003, the company scaled back the pace of openings to concentrate on improving its existing restaurants. That move left more money available for shareholders. In September 2003, it announced a 70% increase in the distribution from $0.235 to $0.40 per share, a step that pushed the payout ratio from the midteens to the 30% level. It has since moved up to the 50% mark.

Did the shift to a higher payout ratio hurt McDonald's growth rate, as the financial theory crowd would have us believe? Not at all. From 1980 through 2002, the last year of the lower payout, McDonald's increased its dividends at an annual rate of 12.3%. Not too shabby. (In that same period, the company's share price gained at an annual rate of 13.1%. *Share prices follow the dividend.*) Since 2003, using the higher level 2003 payment of $0.40 as the base, the dividend has grown at a compound rate of 27.5% to its current level of $2.80 per share. That's even better. And even over this relatively short period, the MCD share price has continued to follow the dividend trajectory. From the end of 2003 through 2011, the annual price appreciation has been 19%, falling somewhat short of the dividend trajectory as the yield has increased, but still reasonably close. (In short measurement periods—and several years is a short measurement period—it is unrealistic to expect dividend and share price to march in lockstep, but over longer measurements, they do correlate closely. These are, after all, real-world businesses.)

From a total return perspective, the story is much the same. From the end of 1980 through the end of 2002, MCD offered investors an annual total return of 13.6%, and that included a nearly 40% drop in the share price in the final year of the measurement period. From the end of 2002 through 2011, the annual total return figure was 25.7%. Even if we take the starting point as the end of 2003—during the course of that year, the MCD shares quickly rebounded from their sharp fall in 2002—the annual total return is still a very impressive 22.3%. In this case, the rise in the payout ratio is not associated with slower growth or lower returns but with higher growth and higher returns. According to modern portfolio theory, that can't be. But here it is all the same.

It Also Adds Down: The Case of Pitney Bowes (and Avon), or Companies That "Can't"

Let me bookend the admittedly unfair comparison of Japan Tobacco and Landauer with another unfair comparison between McDonald's and Pitney Bowes (PBI), the manufacturer of mail franking machines and provider of other mailroom services. If Japan Tobacco had the cash to pay a higher dividend but chose not to, Pitney Bowes is in the opposite position. It has a clear commitment and management inclination to pay a high and rising dividend, but it no longer has the wherewithal to do so. Simply put, its core business is slowly going away. We won't linger on that point much, but I do want to show once again the correlation between a company and its dividend trajectory.

Sales growth over the past two decades has been anemic at best, a 2.3% annual growth rate (see Figure 3.13). Periodic acquisitions have kept the reported results from being even worse. At the same time, margins have been tracking down. As a result, profits have stagnated.

In the meantime, the company has been good to its word, keeping the dividend and even increasing it modestly (see Figure 3.14). That's the type of commitment dividend investors like to see. But there is only so much you can do. The

FIGURE 3.13   Pitney Bowes annual sales growth and operating margin

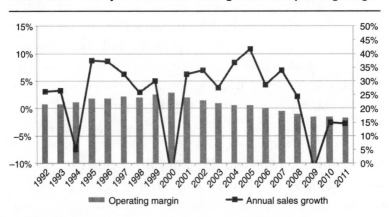

Source: FactSet Research Systems and Federated Investors, 2012.

FIGURE 3.14   Pitney Bowes DPS and payout ratio

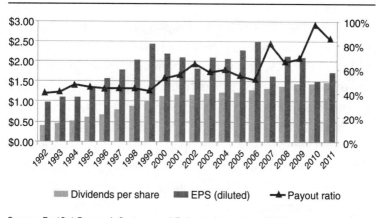

Source: FactSet Research Systems and Federated Investors, 2012.

payout ratio continues to climb, and it appears that the lines are about to cross, as the payout ratio nears 100%. In terms of paying its dividend, Pitney Bowes has had to run faster and faster just to stay in place.

As a businessperson making investments through the stock market, I generally applaud companies that have the courage to have a high payout ratio, but even the most ardent dividend investors want to see a payout that is sustainable. If the company's operations simply cannot support a distribution into the out-years, then the math of the DDM doesn't work, and it's not an attractive investment. That state of affairs is reflected in the company's total return. Pitney Bowes share price is right about where it was 20 years ago. So price appreciation is nil. The company has paid and increased dividends over the past two decades (from $0.39 in 1992 to $1.50 currently), and those dividends have generated all of the company's 81% return to shareholders (from the end of 1992 through 2011). In this instance, a stock market–oriented observer might point out that PBI seems to contradict one of the main tenets of this book, that over the long term a company's share price will follow its dividend trajectory. I would say not so fast. In 1992, the company's stock had a dividend yield of 2%. It currently yields over 10%. In a market that's yielding only 2%, and with the company's stock price falling steadily, investors don't seem to believe that the $1.50 annual payment is sustainable. While it may not be the case that the dividend is cut back to $0.39, in which case the share price and dividend would be trued up at flat exactly, if the dividend is cut, it is necessarily going to bring the payment trajectory a lot closer to the flatlined share price. Depending on where the dividend ultimately ends up, it could still well be the case that the relationship between dividend and share price will assert itself. The jury is still out.

As this book went to print, the jury came in on Avon (AVP), and the verdict was unanimous: share prices follow the dividend. Formerly a member of the Nifty Fifty—stocks from the early 1970s that were to be bought regardless of the price—Avon has struggled in recent years with its distinct, direct-selling business model. Reflecting those headwinds, Avon's share price fell from a high of $44 before the financial crisis in 2008 to $15 by the end of 2012. But the company was able to pay and modestly increase its dividend throughout. Until it wasn't. On November 1, 2012, the board bowed to circumstances and announced a 74% reduction in its distribution. After the cut, the compound annual growth rate for the dividend from 1962 to the present (50 years) fell to 4.4%, which is *not coincidentally* very much in line with the compound annual growth rate of the share price, 4.2%.

We usually say that the share price *follows* the dividend as the ultimate measure of a company's worth. And in the long term, that is clearly the case. In the short term, however, investors may well be ahead of the dividend in pricing the business, in either direction. That is, investors can push up a share price in expectation of a large dividend increase. In Avon's case, as its troubles mounted, stock market investors increasingly came to doubt that Avon would be able to maintain its previously high level of payment. And at the end of the day, they were correct, and the dividend ended more or less where the market pricing indicated it would.

Finding numerous other examples of large, publicly traded companies that have had flat or negative valuation trajectories over a long period is actually quite difficult. The market is efficient over longer measurement periods, and businesses that can't remain truly profitable—in the sense that they can afford to distribute their profits—just don't last very long. And the data soon follows them. Like Pitney Bowes and Avon, they have to be caught in the act, while we still have a paper trail. History, it is said, is written by the victors, and it is certainly true that the victors leave better data sets.

So How Did We Get to This Situation?

But perhaps we should ask, were the industry leaders prior to the 1980s who sent out large profit-sharing checks just—do we say it plainly?—dolts, who should have invested more in their businesses? That is, maybe financial theory, past history, and everyday business practice are just plain wrong. Over a quarter century of declining payout ratios and yields suggests that this is the case. From the mid-1980s through 2011, the dividend payout ratio of the S&P 500 Index fell from the mid-50% range to below 30%. The market's yield fell from around 4% to below 2%. During this period, the market rose steadily, as did earnings. In the late 1990s, the trend accelerated. Though earnings continued to advance, the market went up even faster, and the market's P/E expanded sharply. Investors were willing to pay more (cash) for less (cash). As long as the share prices continued to rise, investors did not perceive the shift away from cash payments to be a problem. The last decade of this experiment in "cashless" return has worked out quite differently. The market has "crashed" twice and is roughly where it was 10 years ago. And in the absence of a material dividend from the S&P 500 Index over that long decade, the market's total return has been unimpressive, a miserly 2% or so per year coming from those scant dividend payments.

Where did those undistributed profits go? They went to share repurchase programs and to mergers and acquisitions. In theory, both should have boosted EPS, share repurchases by lowering the share count and timely, well-priced acquisitions by boosting a business's growth and profit profile. How did that work out? As you can see from Figure 3.15, the growth in profits per share of the S&P 500 Index didn't necessarily get much better, but it certainly became a great deal more volatile.

FIGURE 3.15   S&P 500 Index annual earnings growth

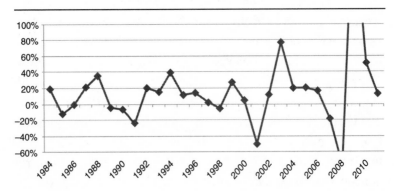

Source: Data from www.econ.yale.edu/~shiller/data.htm and Federated Investors, 2012.

So did the market itself. Having traded in those steady, boring quarterly payments in favor of exciting price-dominated returns, investors got exactly that: lots of movement. If you like roller coasters, you should have enjoyed being a stock investor the past 20 years. The 1990s featured a steep ascent, up 220% from the end of 1994 to the end of 1999, followed by a gut-wrenching "correction" during which the S&P 500 Index fell by 48% from its early 2000 peak to its trough in October 2002. The carriages of the roller coaster ascended again on the back of the financial and housing bubble late in the last decade, during which the market doubled (from October 2002 to October 2007). Then you got to enjoy another off-the-precipice drop of 56% in the aftermath of the financial crisis. That was more than the first loop-the-loop, and far more than what you should experience from investing in S&P 500 Index companies. Since the March 2009 low, the S&P 500 Index has more than doubled to its September 2012 peak.[11] Dramamine, anyone? The market is currently just about where it was over one decade ago. Are we poised for another drop? I don't know. I do know that as a child I never liked roller coasters. As an adult, I like them even less. Higher payout ratios might not have prevented the dot-com bubble or the more recent financial crisis, but the low payout ratios that we've seen in recent decades have clearly played a contributing role to the stock market's high level of volatility.

Lower Cash Returns, Higher Volatility, Lots of Wastage, a Lousy Business Model

So what were the consequences of the shift from a 50% dividend payout ratio to a 30% level and the rise of share repurchase programs over the past three decades? First and foremost, investors have seen much lower cash returns from the main part of the market, a very unimpressive 2% or so annual return for nearly the past 15 years. That's a low return in any context, but it is particularly unsuitable when the United States is in the midst of an income drought and when the thirst for income from retiring baby boomers is growing every day. Second, unmoored from the steady return pattern of a meaningful quarterly dividend payment, the stock market has become a much more lively place. The problem is that given the business profile of the main section of the market, it shouldn't be that lively at all. But without a substantial dividend payment, investors on Main Street have had to ride the roller coaster of the market, even when invested in Main Street companies that could and should be sending out a high and gently rising stream of profit-sharing checks. Are you enjoying the ride? Wall Street brokerages and hedge funds are, but are you? Third, the lower payout ratio has left a lot of your money in the pockets of corporate managers. And I'm sorry to say, they've wasted much of it, some by paying too much for acquisitions when that overpayment has been partially facilitated by having piles of cash on hand. But most of it has been wasted in another manner: at the casino. Rather than send you the quarters that have been piling up in the profit bucket, corporate managers have been feeding them into one-armed bandits known as share repurchase programs. Who knows? Perhaps one day they will hit 7-7-7 with your money. Finally, what's wrong with this picture? Well, it's just unbusinesslike, unless your business is working on Wall Street. Then it is very much an excellent business. But if you are an investor, or a large-company corporate executive, or a company board member who actually sees through the glamour of the "stock" market to the reality of investment returns driven by and necessarily dominated by cash payments, having a low cash return from large, mature businesses makes no sense.

What's the Right Payout?

Why should the S&P 500 Index companies have an aggregate payout of 50%? Isn't that an arbitrary figure? Yes, it is. In fact, I would argue that there would be no harm in it being higher, say, the two-thirds payout Benjamin Graham suggested as appropriate more than a half century ago for the rapidly growing industrial corporations of his age. And as the money could come directly from the cash currently wasted on share repurchase programs (and to some extent, large-scale M&A), the redirection of company profits to company owners would not deprive the United States' leading corporations of capital for future investment and growth. (Just shifting the funds used for share repurchases in 2011 to dividends would have raised the payout ratio to over 70 percent for that year, with not one penny less spent on research and development.) So while a 60% or 70% payout would be preferable, 50% would still be a marked improvement over today's 30% payout. And after a three-decade drop in the dividend payout ratio, it may be easier to convince board members to get back to the previous average payout ratio of 50% in the decades before the Great Retreat rather than go for the higher 60% or 70% figure. In short, the current situation is simply inexcusable. Any increase would be welcome, be it to 50%, 60%, or 70%.

And remember, this would be for the S&P 500 Index companies taken together. Within that realm, there would still be room for individual companies to have lower or no payouts—those genuinely growing and needing their profits to continue to expand operations, and those that for whatever reason simply could not sustain a higher payout due to the volatility of their businesses. These would likely occur among materials companies, faddy retailers, highly cyclical industrials, and those that have fallen on hard times. Other factors would also necessarily come into play when considering the appropriate payout ratio: debt levels, off-balance-sheet liabilities, varying pension obligations, and so forth.

Figure 3.16 shows the current median dividend payout for each GIC (global industry classification) sector of the S&P 500 Index (as of December 31, 2011). Keep in mind that these are not averages, but median figures—the payout ratio where half of the payouts are above this number and half are below. As such, the medians are not influenced by a single or even a few outliers that may pay a very large dividend or pay a very small one. Instead, the medians capture what is typical of companies in the sector. And in that regard, the numbers are appallingly low for all but a few sectors.

Let's start with the telcos, which have the highest payouts. The actual telco figure, off the chart here at 260.6%, reflects several factors. First, there are only eight phone companies in the S&P 500 Index,[12] and several of the landline-only vendors have, by design, payouts of net income above 100%

FIGURE 3.16   S&P 500 Index median dividend payout ratios

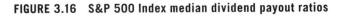

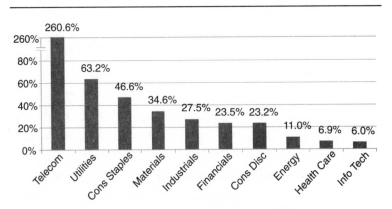

Source: FactSet Research Systems and Federated Investors, 2012.

but well below their free cash flow generation. (This is discussed in *The Strategic Dividend Investor*.) Second, AT&T (T) and Verizon (VZ), the behemoths of the industry, took very large non-cash pension accounting charges—investors can't get away from them!—in 2011 that reduced their net income. Their dividends remained intact, in fact went up several percent, so the impact on the payout ratio was that it skyrocketed. A more typical payout for AT&T, Verizon, and the others in the sector would be in the 70% to 80% payout range, quite appropriate for their GDP growth profile.

Utilities come in second at 63% and could be higher, but given the capital expenditure plans that they have over the next decade, it is probably prudent that they not revert anytime soon to the 85% level proposed by Benjamin Graham in his *Security Analysis*. Consumer staples rank third with a 47% payout, but that is skewed higher by the tobacco companies, which distribute 80% or so of their profits. Ex-tobacco, the staples would have around a 40% payout, which is attractive given the numbers for other sectors but still low on an absolute level. Taking into account the stability and general predictability of their businesses, their payouts should be higher, in the 50% to 60% range.

Next in line is the materials group. This used to be a much larger portion of the S&P 500 Index, and the entire sector is somewhat of a vestige of an earlier, more industrial age. The payout ratio for these companies will vary depending on where they are in their particular commodity cycle. Sometimes it will be high; sometimes it will be low. It would be inappropriate to expect too much from this group. Fortunately, it represents only a small percentage, less than 5%, of the S&P 500 Index at present.

Financials, consumer discretionary, and industrials are all bunched around the level of a one-quarter payout. Most of the large financial institutions are currently constrained by regulatory authorities from having a payout above 30%, but the financials as a whole didn't distribute enough even before they got into trouble.[13] As for consumer discretionary, those managers claim they need to hold onto their cash for a rainy day. That may be so, but in the meantime, company owners are held hostage to the weather forecast that always seems to threaten showers. That's not a very attractive proposition for long-term investors. In the argot of our business, consumer discretionary names are a "trade" rather than businesses to own. There's nothing wrong with that, but the fly-by-night nature of many of them should give long-term investors pause. Industrials can claim to face the same challenge—the cyclicality of their businesses—but during the heyday of U.S. manufacturing a half century ago, these companies supported much higher payout ratios. They could do it again. Now they seem to prefer supporting the brokerage industry. While U.S. industrials spent $31 billion in dividends in 2011, they wasted $42 billion in share repurchases in the same 12-month period. U.S. industrials clearly aren't sitting on the cash for a rainy day. This sector can clearly afford a higher payout ratio; 50% may be too much to ask for, but 28% is just too low.

Energy, healthcare, and information technology bring up the rear, with median payouts of between 6% and 11% in 2011. It is true that energy companies are subject to notable volatility in their businesses—oil at $80 per barrel one day, $140 per barrel a few months later, and then back to $80 again. And the industry currently faces huge outlays to invest in further exploration and production. That's a given. In their case, it may be sufficient just to turn off the share repurchase spigot and shift those funds to dividends. In 2011, S&P 500 Index companies in the energy space spent $44 billion on share repurchases compared to $27 billion in dividends. Without compromising their capex budgets or even their M&A opportunities, firms in this space could more than double the amount of money distributed to company owners. Indeed, the median payout doesn't really tell the whole story in the energy patch, which is dominated by one company. ExxonMobil (XOM) alone could transform the financial returns of the industry. It currently pays $9 billion in dividends per year, one-third of the industry total. It also misallocated $22 billion of cash into share repurchases in 2011. That's one-half of the industry total. If ExxonMobil were to distribute those profits, the industry's aggregate payout of profits would nearly double from $27 billion to $49 billion. That would not change the median payout much— ExxonMobil is just one of 42 energy companies in the S&P 500 Index—but it would increase the aggregate industry payout from 22% to 40%, a much more reasonable number.

The same imbalance of payments is observed in the health-care sector. While the median payout is a scanty 7%, the payout of aggregate profits is higher—35%—due to giants Johnson & Johnson (JNJ), Pfizer (PFE), Merck (MRK), Lilly (LLY), Bristol-Myers Squibb (BMY), and Abbott Laboratories (ABT). These six companies accounted for $25 billion or 80% of the sector's $31 billion in dividends in 2011. The remaining 46 companies in the space paid little if anything in dividends. Their total was $6 billion. But these remaining companies were able to find $47 billion to spend on share repurchases that year. My point is simple: opponents of a shift back in favor of higher dividends will claim that such a move would come at the expense of investment. My answer is that it would not. Just redirecting the funds used for share repurchases back to their rightful owners—shareholders— would raise the payout, benefit shareholders, and not hurt the companies.

Information technology is right up there (down there?) with healthcare in having a single-digit median payout. I've kept it for last because in a tech-crazed world in which everyone wants to cash in on that hot IPO and sell their company to Google, it's important to slow down, step back, and look at the capital allocation policies for companies that make up just under one-fifth of the S&P 500 Index. Some of these companies are equipment manufacturing enterprises that are inherently cyclical and could reasonably justify keeping a little cash set aside for a downturn, but the rest are service and software companies that have a high percentage of recurring revenues and the ability to reward company owners for their wisdom. Could anyone seriously argue that taking the dividend payout ratio up to 20% or 30% or 40% would really slow the development of information technology in our society? I doubt it.

Of the pitiful $24 billion paid in dividends by companies in this sector in 2011, half came from just three companies: Microsoft (MSFT) ($5.2 billion), Intel (INTC) ($4.1 billion), and IBM (IBM) ($3.5 billion). (Alas, those three firms spent more than three times that on share repurchases: $41 billion.) But what of the other 69 technology companies in the index? Remember, these are S&P 500 Index members. They are not start-ups struggling to make payroll. Indeed, they enjoyed a combined net income of $109 billion in 2011. Of that amount, they paid out just $11.1 billion in dividends. Not surprisingly, given the casino-like atmosphere surrounding their share prices, they spent much more, $54 billion, on buying back company stock. Keep in mind that share repurchases in the technology space really are a form of executive and employee compensation, and as long as the dividend investor realizes that the "non-cash" share compensation shown on the income statement is in fact very much a cash outlay because it drives significant real money outflows from the company's bank account in the form of share repurchases, he or she can make a judgment as to the attractiveness of investments in the sector.

Given the skimpy yields and the rampant capital misallocation, however, there's not much to choose from. Intel and some of the other chip manufacturing companies are notable exceptions, with relatively high payout ratios and attractive dividend yields despite operating in a cyclical business. Were Microsoft to raise its dividend payout ratio materially, the recurring nature of its profit stream could also be of interest to the dividend investor. As for the rest, they are "trades." Good luck with that.

Conclusion

We noted earlier that share repurchases can lead to nominal earnings per share growth for the company engaged in the buyback. In some cases, the contribution from share repurchases can be substantial. For instance, consider the case of Lorillard, Inc. (LO), the third largest cigarette maker in the United States and a company that has been operating continuously since 1760. Having been spun off from the Loew's Corporation in 2008, the company has been buying back stock at a good clip. From 2009 through 2011, the company bought back $3.2 billion in shares, reducing the share count in that period by just over 20%. During this period, net income gained 26%, but due to the share repurchases, EPS rose at a higher rate of 55%. That is, over half of the EPS gains can be attributed to the repurchase activity. Through the first three quarters of 2012, the company's operating profit was flat, but EPS rose another 6% due to continued share repurchases. In effect, *all* of the "growth" in that measurement period came from financial engineering. That is, in those cases where share count is reduced, and debt isn't too expensive, and the purchases aren't ill-timed, etc., etc., the math works.

At the aggregate S&P 500 Index level, however, ongoing share issuance and the poor timing of the repurchases at the individual company level have meant that the programs have not really helped the overall market's earnings in a material fashion. Studies of share repurchases suggest no clear trend, concluding that some years buybacks helped the market's overall EPS modestly, in other years concluding that dilution from share issuance was greater. If the share repurchase spigot were turned off, it is possible though not certain that the market would face a one-time earnings headwind. So be it. Perhaps that "shock" would lead to a moment of realization by investors of the extent to which some of their companies have been "growing" through artifice rather than through genuine expansion. And keep in mind that this potential slowdown in EPS growth would be offset at the total return level (dividend plus share price movement) by the greater cash payment.

Let me end this chapter with a simple observation: coming to the conclusion that S&P 500 Index companies should pay robust dividends is not an exercise in rocket science. It is noting a basic business proposition, in favor of the proper distribution of a reasonable share of company profits (net income) to company owners (shareholders). For publicly traded companies, that means dividends. Wall Street and, I'm afraid to say, corporate America make it much more complicated than it needs to be. In the next chapter, I want to suggest some solutions that would help align the interests of Wall Street and Main Street when it comes to the disposition of those corporate profits.

4

In God We Trust, All Others Pay Cash

Throughout this work, and in *The Strategic Dividend Investor*, I have emphasized that investors should look through the stock market to see the underlying enterprises available for ownership there and take the view that they are not just holders of the stocks but owners of said businesses. To drive that point home, I have often referred to local or small companies—whose shares are unlikely to be traded on an exchange and who therefore are more likely to be viewed properly as businesses, not the playthings that stocks have become. On the other hand, I have been equally consistent in my criticism of the poor capital allocation in the "market," defined as the S&P 500 Index of the largest corporations in the United States. But those two arenas—that of local business on one hand and corporate giants on the other—are not the same, and to understand how we've gotten into a situation where the biggest and most successful companies in the country have come to adopt a most "unbusinesslike" stance in regard to capital allocation, we need to return to the previous discussion of the differences between small and large enterprises.

In an earlier chapter, I pointed out that as an analytical exercise, the overall approach to IBM and Johnny's lawn-mowing business should be roughly the same. Here I want to delve into how they are different, and how a universally accepted business proposition—that large, mature, modestly growing companies should be in a position to make significant profit distributions to company owners—was *reversed* by the time it got to the pinnacle of the U.S. business pyramid. Understanding how that misallocation of capital happened will make it much easier to identify the path to correct it. The proposed solution goes beyond simply expecting corporations to increase their profit distributions because it is the right thing to do from a financial perspective; the solution also involves elements of culture and the structure of relationships within our society. Assertions about those realms are necessarily subjective, and in that vein, this chapter doesn't have any charts or tables, and just a little data. While it reaches back to developments four centuries ago, the main point is about the future. I don't claim to have a perfect answer to the "problem" of the stock market—the misallocation of $3 trillion away from shareholders over the last decade, and the damage that has done to the reputation of America's leading corporations—but as a professional investor, I do want to point out ways that corporate America might at least partially address the situation and perhaps return to the good graces of the public. We are well past the "what's good for GM is good for America" stage—that love affair is most certainly over—but it is still possible to imagine a situation in which Main Street roots for corporate America to do well and stands to benefit from the latter's good fortune. That's almost a radical notion these days, but the suggestions that follow could play a small role in bringing large U.S. corporations back into the public's favor.

Owner Versus Operator

By now you are quite used to me stating that to invest successfully, one needs to step back from the stock market to see the businesses behind the stocks. Here we need to take an additional step back and examine the underlying corporate structure of the businesses we propose to own. That structure holds the key, I would argue, to understanding how we got to our current state of affairs and how we might improve it. As most of you already know or could easily imagine, the public ownership of big business is a relatively recent phenomenon. It developed over the course of the last two centuries and emerged from the confluence of economic, cultural, and legal factors that characterized Western Europe starting in the early stages of the Industrial Revolution in the eighteenth and early nineteenth centuries. (Some historians would want to push that starting point back several centuries earlier to Italian merchant practices during the Renaissance or to the medieval craft guilds or even further back into antiquity. They are welcome to do so. The analysis here is limited to the "breakout" phase of modern capitalism, and that clearly dates from the eighteenth century.) Prior to that time, businesses, as one would expect, were smaller, family affairs. Most people were engaged in agricultural pursuits in one form or another and had a very limited scope of activity. To the extent that individuals had an opportunity to operate independently and to seek something beyond a subsistence existence, their craftwork or trading or light manufacturing operations were family based and if possible would be passed on to the next generation of family members. The business could get as large as the family, but not much larger. And should the family disagree or splinter, the business would as well. These types of enterprises still exist widely today. It is the owner-operator model, with the business owner also serving as the key decision maker and executive. The owner operates the business; the operator owns the business. The interests of the two are aligned. The owner-operator might not always make good business decisions, but there is no underlying fundamental conflict of interest or loss of understanding between owner and operator because they are one and the same. In an extended family operation, disagreements might arise over the business, but they would be disagreements among the owner-operators.

You don't have to look much beyond your local dry cleaner, the plumber, your family's dentist, a nearby farmer, the local franchisee of a national quick-service restaurant, rental property owners in your neighborhood, or perhaps your own company (and let's not forget Johnny's lawn-mowing business) to see the owner-operator model in action. (Modestly sized partnerships among individuals who are not family members—many law firms, for instance—fit into the same overall category.) In that context, it is not surprising that as the business matures, or as the owner-operator ages, the growth rate slows and the capital needed to be put back into the business diminishes. The owner-operator begins to take larger distributions from the profit pool. It might be called a draw, a dividend, a partnership distribution, or just a higher salary, but it is the same—excess cash from a profitable enterprise gets distributed to the company owner(s).

The owner-operator model is the base structure for just about all new business endeavors and for most ongoing small enterprises. Its shortcoming is singular—it lacks scale. The business cannot get much larger than the family that supports it. Johnny can only be in one place at a time. He can hire other people to assist him, but he can manage only so many people in so many geographies—and trust them to behave as he would. Johnny probably trusts his children (assuming the lawn-mowing business gets that far) and perhaps his siblings to help him manage the company, but truly extended family operations that are able to prosper across geographies and endure over generations—the Rothschilds of Europe come to mind—are the rare exception. Owner-operators are similarly constrained in that they are generally personally liable for any major losses that they may incur in their enterprises. That sobering reality limits the likelihood that owner-operators are going to take on much risk. Even if they wanted to borrow a lot of money to materially expand their operations, they might have a hard time finding someone to lend it to them. Owner-operator businesses have dotted the global landscape for many centuries and continue to do so to this day, but as dots, not broad swathes across the business spectrum.

The key to the scale of operations that we associate with modern global capitalism emerged slowly but made real headway in seventeenth-century Netherlands with the appearance of the Dutch East India Company. Others soon followed. Called joint-stock companies, limited liability companies, corporations, and so forth, they advanced beyond the owner-operator model by allowing individuals to invest in a business without having the obligation of running it. Moreover, those investors were generally liable only for the capital that they put into the business, not for any losses that extended beyond the original money that they put up. This new limited liability environment allowed entrepreneurs to raise amounts of capital that previously would have been unthinkable: these were the large sums needed to build the railroads, shipping lines, and massive industrial plant characterizing nineteenth- and twentieth-century Western economic development. The path to large-scale business had been cleared. While many of these new entities remained "private," those that wanted or needed to raise additional capital from a broader group of investors, or just to permit existing shareholders to "cash out" their stakes, could offer shares to outside investors on the public exchanges that appeared, initially in Western Europe and then elsewhere. The value of these businesses was thus determined daily as individuals bought and sold shares. And so emerged the modern stock market.

Who's in Charge?

How was management of these new corporate structures to be provided once the owner-operator nexus had been broken? In theory, it was (and remains) quite simple: the new entities were overseen by boards of directors that represented the interests of the company owners. Fractional ownership (the existence of many small shareholders) meant that it was impractical to have all company owners vote on every major issue facing a company. Instead, a board of directors would represent the company owners, appoint the hired help (the managers), and meet regularly to review the condition of the company. In the earliest stages of corporate development, board members could be permanent, and they generally were the biggest shareholders. Over time, as ownership of publicly traded corporations became more diffused, board members became subject to periodic election—the very large shareholders get to reelect themselves—and having a big stake (or even any stake at all) no longer seems to be required. Board membership can now include people (academics, public service individuals) who have only a nominal holding at the time of their election. They are brought onto a board for other reasons—for the specific skills or knowledge they offer to the enterprise.

The emergence of modern, large-scale business is a fascinating topic, but in regard to investing for dividends, we need to focus on one consequence in particular: the relationship between owners and operators once the direct link between the two had been broken. In modern business-school lingo, the conflicts, misunderstandings, and other challenges of having someone else do your bidding rather than doing it yourself is considered an "agency cost." You pay others to cut your hair, to fix the plumbing, to build the addition to your house, and to do the dry cleaning because they have the resources and skills to accomplish the task efficiently and, generally speaking, you do not. But it is not a perfect system. The hairdresser may not cut your hair exactly as you imagined, the plumber shows up at his leisure, dealing with the contractor is simply a nightmare, and the drycleaner sometimes loses your trousers. That's life in a complex society. There is a rich literature on the agency costs of modern large corporations, but our concern here is on the specific cost that arises for shareholders in regard to their ownership stake, their share of the profits. And from the perspective of minority investors (that is, not majority owners), the declining dividend payout ratio of U.S. corporations over the past several decades should be viewed as among the highest agency costs encountered when investing in a business through the stock market. That's because the dividend payout ratio didn't come down from 50% to 30% by itself. It was not moved by an act of Congress. Instead, as we investors are told over and over again, the dividend is "set" by the board. During that period, the directors of the S&P 500 Index companies allowed the payout ratio to drop precipitously. (At the same time, the new tech companies emerging on the scene had no or low payouts, even after they had made the transition from start-up to profitable and ongoing.) Those boards either directly or indirectly authorized the use of the funds that previously went to company owners—whom they are supposed to represent—to go to share repurchase programs or large-scale mergers and acquisitions (M&A). This is a classic agency problem.

It turns out that the same developments that several hundred years ago led to large-scale modern enterprises sowed the seeds within them of a conflict of interest whereby the "hired help"—the corporate managers—began to act in a manner that is not in the interest of the company owners. (Hello, Japan Tobacco.) My key point, however, is that corporate boards did little to resist the move away from dividends. The separation of management from ownership can, of course, open the door to all sorts of management malfeasance—Enron, AIG, and their like—but that is quite clearly not the issue here. Instead, it is the *seemingly benign*, multidecade gradual decline in payout ratios for old economy companies and the failure of new economy firms to initiate material profit distributions once those businesses have transitioned from start-up to ongoing. These failures seem innocent enough, but as I have tried to demonstrate in the previous chapters and in *The Strategic Dividend Investor*, the consequences of this shift in capital allocation have been terrible for investors and bad for the companies themselves.

So why have boards of major corporations blessed the use of your money for share repurchase programs and large-scale M&A, both of which are known carcinogens for the investment body? That's an excellent question, and you should pose it yourself to the companies in which you have an ownership stake. Most public corporations list the name of the corporate secretary on their website, and it will certainly be in their regulatory filings with the SEC. Write to them and ask that the question be passed on to the directors. You'll be lucky to get even the slightest reply—"Thank you for your interest in the Acme Widget Company"—but if enough of you write, and if shareholder concern about the shift in capital allocation gets enough attention, perhaps the board might come to examine and reconsider the choices that it has made over the past several decades.

Still, how did we get to this situation? There were many contributing factors, but the multidecade decline in interest rates has played a critical role. Indeed, in 2012, the cash rate of return on the benchmark 10-year Treasury bond hit an *all-time* low of 1.5%. According to modern portfolio theory, low interest rates can be used to justify a low payout and therefore skimpy cash returns from equities. And for many market participants, that has been the case. Too many corporate managers have simply looked at the interest rate structure and come to the conclusion that their low payout and low yield were sufficient, regardless of how unattractive such a yield might be in absolute terms. In a practical sense, that is basically true—companies can get away with offering a low return and still attract capital, despite the fact that this approach can and has been devastating to long-term investor returns.

The CEO and the Board

But that's a mathematical explanation, and it gets you only so far. Indeed, I would argue that the real reason corporate boards have blessed a bad policy has only a little to do with the math. Instead, it is about individuals, relationships, and trust. Let me explain what I mean. The CEO and the other senior executives are appointed by and accountable to the board, who are the representatives of the company owners. That's the theory. In practice, it works out a little differently. Most CEOs of S&P 500 Index companies are hard-charging "alpha" personalities who have gotten to that position because of their success in growing their businesses. And what do CEOs want to do? That which made them CEOs in the first place: to continue to expand the company as fast as possible. That means reinvesting as much as they can, making large acquisitions, and so forth, all in an effort to make have the company become even larger. Having achieved success and been appointed to lead the company, CEOs are inclined to continue on that path, even when it may no longer comport with economic reality. *Few if any large-company CEOs are willing to acknowledge the 5% growth limit, or even if they do, they will state that they are not there yet.* And if there is cash left on the table after all the empire-building measures have been taken, the CEOs are inclined toward using it for share repurchases for all the reasons we reviewed in Chapter 2. It is the rare CEO who willingly accepts the proposition that sending out a larger check to company owners is the appropriate use of the company's excess cash.

Now one can scoff and say that CEOs *should not* be satisfied with the 5% limit, that there is always market share to be taken from competitors, that there are always new businesses to enter and declining businesses to exit. And in that context, all CEOs should aim for much better than GDP. That is true. The result is a Lake Wobegon situation where all the CEOs are above average, at least in their aspirations, but the results are like the world beyond Lake Wobegon, just average. The S&P 500 Index of our nation's leading companies has recorded profit growth over the past half century that in aggregate is not much better than GDP growth in the same period. That's a fact that CEOs and boards need to come to terms with when considering the proper allocation of capital.

Given the organizational dynamic between the CEO and the board, however, directors are as likely as not to go along with what the CEO wants. In the instance when the CEO is brought in from the outside to shake things up, it is even more the case that the board is going to give that individual certain leeway to set capital allocation policies for a number of years. In both instances, the CEO gets his or her way. Moreover, board members turn over periodically. After a CEO has been in place for a while, he or she will have a significant say in who ends up on the board. After a while, it's fair to say that the board can become the CEO's board. The board may be filled with independent directors (a legal description of board members who are formally separate from the company and its executives) but still be "the CEO's board."

That's notable because there is no absolute reason why the "hired help" even needs to be on the board of directors. Of course, it is common that the CEO and sometimes other senior executives would be. And for many younger companies, it makes sense that the leading entrepreneur behind a company would not only be on the board, because he or she still controls much of the stock, but also in effect dominate the board, taking counsel from the other directors but not really being subordinate to them. That's natural and as it should be for those younger companies. It is far less prevalent in the realm of large, more mature corporations such as those that populate the S&P 500 Index. In those instances, the CEO rarely started the company and is equally unlikely to be the largest shareholder. Such CEOs really are the hired help, deserving of respect and support but not a blind check to do as they see fit in all circumstances.

Combine these two factors—the directors relying on the judgment of the CEO and the CEO's role in determining the long-term composition of the board—and you have created an environment in which the payout ratio can and did drift down. Now critics will point out that both of these factors existed earlier when payouts and yields were much higher. And they are correct. So we are back to the question of why boards have blessed the multi-decade drop in dividend payout ratios. Here we do have to circle back to the business environment, which, frankly, was conducive to growth during much of this period. As I've mentioned before, the easiest explanation for the boards to adopt is the one about declining interest rates. By the 1980s, neat and tidy (and ultimately wrong) modern portfolio theory had come to completely dominate boardroom financial thinking. And by that theory, declining interest rates provided plenty of cover for paying out less of the profits to company owners and redirecting that cash elsewhere. The decline in the payout ratio was further assisted by the rise of the share repurchase program as a mass-market phenomenon starting in the mid-1980s and gathering pace through the 1990s. Most of those dollars came out of the pool that had previously gone to dividend payments. In the long bull market from 1982 onward, share repurchases looked smart because share prices were rising steadily.

That the country appeared to be on the path of fairly sustainable growth after an economic funk that lasted 15 years—from the mid-1960s to the early 1980s—also didn't slow down the decline in the payout ratio. Indeed, real economic growth in the 1990s was higher than it had been (and would be) in the periods adjacent to it. In many industries, particularly cyclical and capital intensive ones, high reinvestment rates and temporarily lower dividend payout ratios may have made sense, though we ended up paying for the possibly excessive growth of the 1990s with subpar expansion in the 2000s. In effect, the overinvestment of one decade led to less activity a decade later. Still, even the most ardent dividend investor has to acknowledge that it was a period when large companies could find themselves expanding at a rapid rate. For those businesses that couldn't or didn't enjoy the organic growth of the 1990s, they could buy growth, with debt that got cheaper every year as interest rates fell, or use their inflated shares as currency in all-stock deals. And then the paradigm-breaking technology companies entered the scene. They were not even part of the S&P 500 Index world in the early years of this period (prior to the mid-1990s), but they purported to offer investors a new way of making money—through IPOs of companies at early stages of development followed by meteorically rising share prices—rather than the old fashioned way of cash payments from profitable operations. Dividend payments simply fell out of fashion. Like so many other temporary trends, letting the payout ratio fall at large corporations "seemed like a good idea at the time." Throughout this period, the tax rate on both capital gains and dividend income was coming down, but executives and boards saw what they wanted to see—the former more than the latter—and pushed headlong toward a stock-oriented investment world and away from a dividend-focused one.

It is not the case that all CEOs were and are averse to profit distribution plans, and it is equally unfair to charge all corporate boards with being negligent, but facts are facts: the dividend payout ratio and the cash return on the S&P 500 Index companies have plummeted to levels that make business investment through the main part of the stock market (as opposed to pure speculation) very difficult. And in the corporate structure that got its start 400 years ago and ultimately helped usher in the age of large and easily investible enterprises, the board of directors is ultimately responsible. The buck stops there. The board (and the CEO) can point to all sorts of reasons why their individual cases deserve an exception, and why they are not to blame for the general decline in payout ratios and yields. Yes, yes, and the road to hell, they say, is paved with good intentions. Well, we have arrived. Much of Main Street doesn't trust the stock market—why should they?—and their view of corporate America isn't much better. And the investing public has voted quite clearly with its feet. In recent years, mutual fund flows—a measure of popular investment sentiment—have been strong in one direction: out of equities and into bonds. Surely that is a circumstance that CEOs and directors cannot be happy to see.

Higher Payouts and the Board of Directors

That's the past. Where do we go from here? Some paths are obvious, some less so. The first corrective measure is that the balance of power in corporate America, at least in regard to the dividend payout ratio, needs to move back toward the owners of the companies, through their representatives, the directors. Every year (month, week, day?) brings a new scandalous episode of "corporations gone wild." Greater discipline at the board level about the allocation of capital won't necessarily prevent future scandals from happening, but if you look at the org chart of corporate America, the board is ultimately responsible for how companies operate. Permitting very low payout ratios, embracing large-scale M&A, and endorsing massive and ill-timed share repurchase programs ultimately come from the boardroom. They may be proposed by the executive team, but they have to be approved by the directors. Rather than rubber-stamp those requests from management, corporate boards should look a lot more closely at them than they have in the past. For far too many companies, board membership is viewed as a sinecure for retired executives. It should not be a sinecure under any circumstance, but perhaps the retired executives serving as directors of S&P 500 Index companies can see what the current CEO cannot or does not want to see: that after a certain point, a very high level of reinvestment for large, stable, slow-growing (GDP+/–) corporations amounts to throwing good money after bad. For those companies, excess profits should be distributed to company owners, not via the casino of the stock market but directly as a cash payment.

And here there is some good news to report, if not in regard to the payout ratio itself but in regard to the balance of power in the boardroom: in recent years, the movement to separate the roles of chief executive and chairman of the board has gained speed. One decade ago, approximately a quarter of boards split the responsibilities. In 2011, just over 40% of the S&P 500 Index companies have a chairman who is not the CEO of the company. On its own, that shift is not a big deal and is part of a much larger discussion about corporate governance. But we'll take what we can get. An independent chairman can support bad capital allocation decisions just as readily as the CEO, but by separating the roles, I would like to think that there is a greater chance of the board having a conversation on the topic, rather than everyone simply lining up behind the CEO's spending plans.[1] A recent print advertisement for an executive education program also seems to address the problem of getting balance back into the boardroom. It promoted a "certificate of training" for non–executive directors, those who are not themselves senior officers at the company. The magazine graphic advertising the program caught my attention: it showed a simple seesaw, with five individuals on one side balancing in weight a single person standing on the other side. I suppose it could be read to be about training the one to stand up to the many. But given the current state of the boardroom, I understood that the program could also be about readying the many (the directors) to stand up to the one—the CEO.[2]

Companies will no doubt respond to this criticism by claiming that their boards are very hardworking, take their responsibilities seriously, and come to decisions about capital allocation after in-depth analyses. I would like to believe that, were it not for the past several decades of documented history that suggest just the opposite. But that is all in the past. As we investors will be assured, the board will be looking particularly closely at all capital allocation decisions going forward. In the same way that the board should not micromanage the affairs of the company—they've hired professionals to run it—shareholders should not micromanage the affairs of the directors. Still, as those directors consider the dividend payout issue, may I offer a few observations that should frame those deliberations?

Interest Rates

Continuously declining and then just absolutely really low interest rates have been an easy excuse for all sorts of bad economic and financial decision making in recent years. Weak business plans suddenly become quite viable, on paper, when money is cheap. But no more. Interest rates are at rock-bottom levels. In fact, when adjusted for modestly rising costs (inflation), real interest rates are negative. There are two scenarios from here. If interest rates stay steady at current levels for a long time, it is probably because we are in a prolonged recession or in an extended period of anemic growth. (Think Japan for the past decade or so.) In that environment, large, mature companies should and will come to the conclusion that they are looking at lower returns on incremental business investments. A slow economy is a slow economy, so opening up the new plant or moving into a new territory will make less sense. In that case, the basic profitability of large corporations, particularly those S&P 500 Index behemoths that are not in the cyclical part of the economy, will lead them to having more cash on hand than they need to address new business opportunities. Rather than opt for share repurchases—the last decade's preferred (mis)use of excess cash—or large-scale M&A (I fear the temptation of the next 10 years), they should return the cash directly to shareholders. In an environment of sustained low interest rates, the higher-payout approach would have the additional benefit of helping to meet investors' real-world need for income.

In the second instance, interest rates return to more normal levels where risk is at least somewhat more appropriately priced. That could come from a variety of sources such as inflation kicking in or simply an end to the government's policy of keeping rates artificially low. The thing to keep in mind in a rising-rate environment is that the discount rate applied to future cash flows also starts moving up. The prospective growth rate is also rising, but the discount rate is no less important. In that scenario, the attributes of a cash payment now rather than the prospect of an inflated (and more highly discounted) share price later should be clearer than in the current low-interest-rate, low-discount-rate world. That is, we are in an extreme situation. Whether interest rates stay at the current levels—woe to our economy and society if they do—or move back to more normal levels (a 10-year Treasury bond at 4% or so), it is awfully hard to justify the low dividend payout ratios that corporate America now has.

Outtake: What About Utilities?

Stock market traders will point out here that high-payout utilities "underperform" as stocks in a rising or high-inflation environment and that a higher payout ratio would work "against" the dividend-focused investor when rates are moving up. Indeed, there is some truth to the first part of that statement. Many distribution utilities are regulated businesses with an essentially fixed revenue structure. If inflation becomes significant, they can fall behind on an NPV basis, as it takes time for them to file and get approval for new, higher rates. Many utilities have catch-up mechanisms in place, but even these take time to be implemented. So in periods of high inflation and/or sharply rising interest rates, their profits struggle to keep up compared to the profits of companies that have more pricing power—essentially all businesses that are not on long-term, fixed-price contracts. In addition, ownership of utilities in an inflationary period can appear relatively unattractive because investors can tap into similar if not better cash streams from a wide variety of other sources—corporate bonds, Treasuries, etc.—that may be further up the capital structure or less volatile than common equity. That's all true.

But the challenge that regulated distribution utilities face is perhaps the exception that proves the rule. A return to normal rates of risk—with proper long-term discount rates put into the valuation mechanism—should make investors *more* rather than less attracted to cash payments now rather than relying mostly on the hope that inflation will be reflected in rising share prices that can be turned into lots of cash later through a trade. It's too easy to forget that to derive value from a share price–dominated system (as opposed to a cash payment system), you have to trade. And trading, as the historical record clearly shows, is a very, very hard way to make money. In essence, a bird in the hand is worth two (inflated ones) in the bush. That's the risk of forgoing a dividend payment in an inflationary period. And if the investor is fortunate enough to not need the cash income at that very moment, dividend reinvestment allows one's ownership stake in a business to increase, regardless of the rate environment.

Economic Growth

It's hard to separate interest rates from economic growth. They generally go hand in hand: high rates of growth generate the prospect of inflation (aggregate demand outstripping the supply of goods and services), which in turn leads interest rates up in order to compensate lenders for the fact that the money they are lending out will be worth less in the future when it is paid back. Central banks then jump in to raise the cost of borrowing, which in turn dampens economic activity, slows demand, and ultimately lowers inflation. For the sake of argument, however, we have isolated the interest rate portion—addressed above—in order to take up the growth portion here.

For the 50-year period from 1962 through 2011, the median growth rate for the U.S. economy was 3.1% real (adjusted for inflation) and 6.3% nominal. In retrospect, it was a boon time, part of the great American century, characterized by widespread home ownership, college educations, good jobs, steadily rising living standards, and so forth. I don't want to make too much of *Happy Days* America, but it was a time of relative prosperity after the dual shocks of the Depression and World War II.

I heartily wish and hope that the next 50 years are just as good for the United States. But in their planning, U.S. corporations, particularly those that by their size or business activity are hemmed in by overall U.S. economic growth, should not necessarily assume that the twenty-first century will be as strong as the back half of the twentieth century was. The population is older; many cities, most states, and most certainly the federal government are deeply indebted; and the nation faces structural economic challenges that it did not have coming out of World War II. Ask 10 economists about their growth forecasts for the next decade, and you'll get 10 different answers.

Who knows for certain? But it is prudent to at least acknowledge the possibility that economic expansion—marginal GDP comes from changes in labor (population and hours worked) and changes in productivity—may not increase as much as it has in the past. On the population front, growth has slowed to less than 1% annually, and there is, alas, increasing support for closing the doors to new immigrants. As baby boomers move closer to retirement, hours worked are going down, not up. On the labor productivity side, we've just come off a period of heightened productivity growth for which we can thank the tech crowd. In the 1990s and for the first half of the last decade, the productivity gains were greater than 2% per annum. In recent years, they have been below 2%. Unless you see a new population spurt ahead, unless you expect seniors to return to their cubicles and start working overtime, or unless you are counting on another breakthrough in technology, 3% real growth may well be the upper limit for the next decade or so. And that's being optimistic. The trend line is actually pointing at the 2% mark. Inflation may get the United States back to the 5% to 6% nominal level investors now consider "normal," but if it does, it will be due to a higher portion of inflation and less real growth.

Simple prudence dictates that S&P 500 Index company directors take into consideration the realistic growth prospects of their (large, mature) enterprises when determining the appropriate level of investment and the disposition of company profits. The possibility, and I would argue the high probability, of a lower growth profile over the next decade or so directly and clearly invites an increased dividend payout ratio.

Share Repurchases and Large-Scale M&A

With less demand for capital reinvestment, large corporations will have more cash on hand from the profitability of their core operations. With that cash, they can buy back shares. That will work as poorly in the next decade as it did in the last. I've spent enough ink on that topic in the previous chapters. Another alternative is to use the funds for large-scale M&A. In a slow-growth environment, that will appeal to some corporate planners. And in those areas of the economy where there truly is no expansion or may even be contraction, consolidation among major participants may be economically warranted. Nevertheless, though it is not the topic of comprehensive review here, it is generally acknowledged that large-scale M&A does not work for the buyer. The acquirer ends up overpaying. In most instances, the buyer and seller identify cost "synergies" (cost cutting) that will result from combining the two entities, but the present value of those synergies usually ends up in the pocket of the seller. The promise of "top line" (revenue) synergies, due to cross selling and so forth, is no longer convincing to anyone but the investment bankers and management consultants who need these transactions to support their own top lines.

Outtake: The Kraft Foods Example

If you want an example of a big, slow-growing S&P 500 Index company buying another large enterprise, paying a substantial premium for it, and seeing how that combination was of no material benefit to the shareholders of the acquirer (but was quite beneficial to investment bankers), you need look no further than Kraft Foods' acquisition of Cadbury in early 2010. Kraft paid $18.5 billion at that time to consolidate its position in the global food and confection business. (An astounding $9.5 billion of that was goodwill—the value of the purchase in excess of Cadbury's net assets, including its brands.) Some $40 million was paid to investment bankers advising Kraft on the deal, and $1.5 billion went on the cash integration costs of the two companies. Was it worth it? At the time the deal was announced, investors were told that the combined entity would be able to grow earnings and dividends faster than Kraft would be able to do on its own. Prior to the acquisition, Kraft—which had been spun off from the Philip Morris Companies in a process that began 10 years earlier in 2001—had earned around $2.00 a share for most of the decade, some years below that figure, several years right around that amount. In the two and half years after the deal for Cadbury closed, Kraft was certainly a larger, more complex company, but it still earned around $2.00 per share. The amount in 2010 was somewhat lower, in 2011 it was right at $2.00 per share, and for three-quarters of 2012, the company was on a $2.00 per share run rate. More important, from the time of the acquisition, Kraft investors saw *no* improvement in their cash return. Kraft still paid the $0.29 per share per quarter that it had since 2008—for four straight years. No change, no growth, zippo, nothing. For a company that was going to resolve its growth challenge through an acquisition, something was amiss.

To finance the transaction, Kraft sold its North American pizza business—an operation that had previously been considered one of Kraft's crown jewels, with the DiGiorno, Tombstone, and Jack's brands—to archrival Nestle at what was viewed at the time as a fire-sale price. And then, less than two years after convincing everyone that it had come up with a business marriage made in heaven, Kraft announced in mid-2011 that what it really wanted was a divorce. It was splitting the company in two. One part would focus on North American grocery and would look a lot like the old Kraft before it embarked on a series of acquisitions, including the Cadbury deal announced in 2009 and an earlier purchase of Danone's LU global biscuit business, which it bought for $7.2 billion in cash in 2007. The other part would consist of the global confectionery operations, which would look a lot like a combination of the Cadbury and LU businesses. Purchased three and five years earlier, they were then spun off in 2012. First the buy-ins, then the spin-offs. It makes me dizzy.

I can certainly be accused of cherry-picking my examples to make my point, but I am happy to open the floor to other views: if you can find any serious studies—no McKinsey, Bain, or major Wall Street investment banks, please—showing that large-scale M&A is anything but value destroying to the buyer, please pass it on. I'll be happy to post it to this book's website and update the next edition with that content and an earnest apology to the world's management consultants and investment bankers.

That's all blather. Judge for yourself. The two Kraft entities began trading separately on October 1, 2012. The global confection business, Mondelez International (MDLZ), has been positioned as the food industry's "hare," fast and lean. The North American grocery business, the Kraft Foods Group (KRFT), is being sold to investors as the tortoise, a slow moving, debt-laden "yield play." Time will tell, but if past experience is any guide, the tortoise beats the hare. Check back in 2017 and 2022.

The Dividend

After S&P 500 Index company CEOs and directors realize that they are in a secular, modest growth environment, that share repurchases are a waste of money, and that large-scale M&A isn't much better, perhaps they will come to the conclusion that for a profitable business to simply send out a check to company owners is not such a bad thing after all. But let us have some compassion for these individuals. It will be a bit of an embarrassment for them around the bar at the local CEO and directors club where the condescension will be palpable. You can imagine their "growth company" peers hiding behind their brandy snifters and saying, "Yes, yes, well, what can we say about old Acme Widget? At least it has a high dividend. Yes, it's good for widows and orphans." May I remind you that those high-dividend widows and orphans stocks absolutely trounce the low/no dividend "growth" stocks when it comes to long-term total returns? (Much of *The Strategic Dividend Investor* was dedicated to documenting this.)

Management's primary responsibility—whether it is a small, private company or a large, publicly traded enterprise—is to maximize long-term value for company owners. For start-ups and companies clearly in growth mode, that necessarily entails substantial if not total reinvestment back into the business. But for S&P 500 Index companies, it is not to create ever larger and larger business empires. Instead, managers and board members need to strike the right balance between an appropriate level of investment in the business and the distribution of the remaining cash. That is the way to maximize value for company owners. In short, for those companies at the apex of corporate America, it is time for them to raise their dividend payout ratio to a level—it will vary by company—that takes into account their realistic growth prospects, a proper pricing of risk, and the realization that buying back shares or buying other companies is no substitute for a profit distribution plan to company owners.

There are also other steps that directors can take. They can link senior executive compensation to the payment and growth of the dividend. That is actually a relatively common practice in dividend-friendly Britain. As a practical measure, that would likely mean shifting from granting stock options—which are at odds with dividend payments—to grants of restricted stock that receive the dividend.[3] Such a step would go a long way toward aligning management's natural self-interest with the goals of the shareholders. As with investors, so too with directors and senior executives, the main change would be one of a mindset—in getting them to see the share price as a reflection (and not a terribly important one at that, as it moves around day to day) of the company's underlying health as manifested by its real and tangible cash distributions. The current focus on share price as the starting point and ending point when assessing a publicly traded company's prospects puts the cart before horse. It's time to put them in the right order.

Trust the Directors?

It is my hope that corporate boards will conclude as soon as possible and through their own deliberations that raising the payout ratio is a good idea. Some will suggest that regulating the payout level or regulating other capital allocation processes would be a means of expediting the process. I strongly disagree. You cannot regulate business judgment. And in a free society, you should not try to—making bad decisions is the risk that you take when you engage others in commercial (as well as noncommercial) enterprises. Suing the directors to get them to consider a higher payout ratio won't work either. Directors have a legal responsibility to act in the best interests of the corporation and its shareholders, but defining that "best interest" is rightly left to the directors. Indeed, the "business judgment rule" effectively protects directors from lawsuits as long as they are deemed to be acting in good faith, with loyalty to the company, and giving due care to the matter at hand. Directors embracing share repurchase programs and even large-scale M&A can make the argument that they are acting in the best interests of the company and the shareholders. They are wrong, but it is a matter of bad judgment, not bad faith. According to the Delaware Supreme Court, whence comes much of our corporate legal canon, a court should not "substitute its own notions of what is or is not sound business judgment."[4]

That is now, but nearly a century ago, a court did compel a major corporation to pay out a portion of its cash as a special dividend. The case law has subsequently moved entirely in the opposite direction, but the story is still worth retelling. In 1919, two investors, the Dodge brothers, sued none other than Henry Ford to force him to pay a special dividend out of the retained profits and cash that had built up on the balance sheet of the Ford Motor Company. At the time, the brothers owned around 10% of the common stock of the company. Henry Ford had previously declined to pay a special dividend, claiming that he wanted to sell cars at a loss in order to maximize the distribution of employment and vehicle ownership. That plan would consume the retained profits on hand that the plaintiffs sought. The court found that Henry Ford's intention to run the company at a loss was inappropriate and ordered him to pay the special dividend.[5] The "backstory" is that the Dodge brothers were building up their own automotive business and wanted the dividend so that they could better compete with Ford. Ford understood this and tried to starve them of capital. In the end, the Dodge brothers got their dividend and built up their own enterprise. Ford did not suffer too much. But it is a tale of high capitalist intrigue, centered on what in corporate America is now considered a lowly item—the dividend. But prior to dividends falling out of favor starting in the past few decades, they were a serious matter, serious enough to dispute in court.

Ultimately, the decision to become a minority shareholder in a corporation comes down to trust. For all the paperwork, for all the small-print disclosures, for all the legal rights, a very basic human relationship—that of trust—is still at the heart of the structure of large, publicly traded corporations, the flippant title of this chapter notwithstanding. The current preference in the United States to have business judgment determined by regulators or made primarily to avoid lawsuits can hardly be considered an improvement over the trust model. If the people acting on your behalf don't warrant your trust, you will find someone else to get the job done— replace the directors. In regard to S&P 500 Index companies where ownership is very diffused, general meetings of the shareholders occur only annually, and directors' terms may be staggered over several years, the idea of "just replace the directors" may not always be a practical solution. The stock market, however, offers the opportunity for company owners to shift their stakes easily from those companies where the trust has not been earned to those where they believe it will be. By doing so, investors effectively raise the cost of capital for those companies that are sold off in the marketplace and lower the cost of capital for those companies whose directors appear to be making prudent decisions. But it is a two-way street. Directors can ask investors to trust them, but directors need to deliver the goods to the people that they represent— the shareholders. From where I'm sitting, well aware of both the historical benefits of higher payout ratios to total return as well as the mathematical challenges encountered by mature companies that do not make profit distributions to company owners, the reason too many investors and would-be investors on Main Street hold a dim view of the large companies traded on the stock market is clear: the cash payment stream for taking a stake in those companies is insufficient. Having the directors get the dividend payout ratio back to where it belongs would be a major step in the direction of earning the trust of the current company owners and getting new ones to join their ranks.

If boards don't step up, others will. Private equity, corporate raiders, and activist investors bring with them a multitude of their own problems, but they are good at one thing—identifying what they believe to be misallocated capital. And while in some instances they contributed to the Great Retreat, they could now be part of the reversion to more normal capital allocation practices. Once they sense that the share repurchase gig is up, that it has gone on too long, they will move in quickly and pressure those companies sitting on large cash hoards or wasting their cash in the stock market. The sooner the directors of low-payout S&P 500 Index companies come to the same realization, the more likely their enterprises and their shareholders will benefit from the resumption of a dividend-focused stance. And those directors will face less pressure from outsiders who would remove them from the boardroom.

Here, Have This Exploding Cigar!

To the best of my ability, I have argued that investors should seek out dividend streams and that corporate America needs to pay higher dividends than it currently does. From the narrow perch of a professional investor, my job is done. Or is it? In the few remaining pages, I want to offer up some ideas associated with the shift back to a higher payout ratio from S&P 500 Index companies and a more meaningful cash return from those investments. But the matter is not limited to just investment returns; it once again comes down to trust.

If the shareholder-director link is an existing trust relationship that could use some repair, there is another trust relationship that could benefit as well and in the same manner: the balancing act that exists between large companies and their employees. I would argue that increasing employee ownership of dividend-paying company stock would go a long way toward facilitating improved relationships between the management and the workforces of big, publicly traded companies. That's not the case currently, at least concerning stock ownership. Too many employee stock ownership plans in recent decades have been the exploding cigars of finance. It's been a gift that you did not want to get. In those instances, by the time employees received shares or representation on the board (in the case of industrial unions), it was too late. Just recall the U.S. auto industry, the U.S. steel industry, airlines on the verge of bankruptcy, airlines coming out of bankruptcy, airlines about to reenter bankruptcy. And then there were the Enron-like 401(k) plans filled with company stock whose value disappeared almost overnight. In short, you don't have to look too far to find numerous other examples of why many employees have little reason to be attracted to having a stake in the company that employs them. Layer over that the century-long history of hostility between "capital" and "labor," and employee ownership of even a bit of stock is a hard sell. Industrial unions aren't the presence that they once were in the United States, but where they are still a force—in old economy industrial enterprises, landline telecommunications, and so forth—the relationships are as bad as ever.

The one exception is in the information technology (and now social networking) space, where employees have historically had broad access to options and shares as well as a sense that the workers are company owners. But keep in mind that options do not entitle investors to the dividends until they actually become shares, and tech company shares generally do not pay dividends in any case. And for all those Google billionaires, there are plenty of employees who watched their shares in the dot-com darlings go to zero when the tech bubble burst a decade ago. So more often than not, whether in the old economy or the new, employees have been given (or been asked to pay for) little pieces of paper that generate little to no cash and often have highly volatile values in the marketplace.

More broadly one could argue that the same mistrust extends beyond the employee-employer relationship and helps explain why general stock ownership among the middle class in this country is as narrow as it is. Just around 50% of families have historically had direct or indirect stock ownership. (In recent years, that figure may have dropped as Main Street investors have fled equities in favor of bonds.) That is a shame. Stock ownership should be much broader. Of course, for basic affordability reasons, share ownership is also relatively narrow. Buying a business—even just a small stake in one—costs money and is beyond the reach of many families, but where there is discretionary cash, stock ownership could be greater for the middle class and could make at least some inroads into the working class. That notion may be jarring. Over the past several decades for too many Americans, stock ownership has gotten a bad rap. Rather than benefit from the steady payment of dividends (and appreciation in value) of successful corporations, investors and would-be investors are barraged by headlines about the gyrations in the share prices of Facebook, Groupon, and their ilk. Even in the absence of scandal, the stock market that many investors experience through their 401(k) plans is remote at best from any sense of being a company owner and getting a slice of the profit pie. Instead, it's all about share prices and beating the stock market. Even if the main part of the U.S. stock market were to revert to a more normal dividend orientation, it would challenge investors with a lot of volatility—share prices do move up and do move down, but nowhere near as much as the casino highs and lows that we have come to know over the past few decades.

Instead of having its current connotation, stock ownership could and should be viewed as an amazing institution
characteristic of a free and open society. The arguments in
favor of broad-based stock ownership should be self-evident:
the opportunity to become an owner of companies whose
goods and services you use every day, the liquidity, the limited
liability, the claim on a real-world asset, the ability to take
a small, affordable stake, and so forth. The case for having
most large-company employees have at least a small dividend-
paying claim on their own enterprise is even stronger: That
dividend stream is a tangible reflection of the state of the company. It is a profit-sharing plan that surely would contribute
to managing relations in the firm and getting everyone to pull
in the same direction. It creates the opportunity to resurrect,
if just in a minor way, the owner-operator model.

Employee Stock Ownership: Revisiting the Ideas of Louis Kelso

In regard to advocating more employee stock ownership (and
by derivation, broader general ownership), I make no claim
to originality. Most of these points have been made by others.
For instance, 50 years ago Louis Kelso urged much higher
dividend payouts and much broader stock ownership as part
of his plan for Universal Capitalism—his answer to the challenge of midcentury state socialism emanating from the Soviet
bloc, on the one hand, as well as his dissatisfaction with the
notion of a blasé and often indifferent Affluent Society world-
view that characterized the wealthy in the 1960s. Kelso went
on to create what we now know as employee stock option
plans, or ESOPs. What is most notable about his take on
the stock ownership "problem" is the role of the dividend. In
his mind, employees would be able to buy company shares
because the scheme would be self-financing from the dividends that corporations paid. Those dividends, *those mate-*

rial dividends, would be used to pay off the loans raised by the ESOPs to buy the shares in the first place. But the entire scheme simply falls apart if the companies have low or no payouts. In his manifesto on the topic, Kelso wrote:

> *We propose that each mature corporation . . . pay out all of its net earnings, after depreciation and operating reserves only, to its stockholders. The right of the owner—the stockholder—to receive all the net income produced by what is owned is the essence of private property. To withhold the wages of capital is no more justifiable than to withhold the wages of labor. Stated affirmatively, the flow of purchasing power to those who engage in producing wealth is just as disrupted by corporate management's withholding the wages of capital (corporate net earnings) as it would be were the wages of labor withheld.*[6]

Corporations could "afford" to have 100% payouts because they would still be able to raise capital by issuing new shares to the employees and from other, nonemployee investors.

Kelso's works are redolent of the "social science" approach to resolving the challenges of the 1960s and 1970s. Nearly 50 years on, they also read as dramatic and naive, not least because of his notion that with 100% payouts, dividend yields would be exceptionally high. Those high yields would permit the ESOPs to pay off their loans very quickly. But there is a kernel of truth in what Kelso wrote, and it focuses on the virtue of wider ownership of equities by employees (and nonemployees) and the idea that those equities of mature companies would naturally have a cash distributive function. Or to put it another way, whether it is organized or not, labor loves profit-sharing plans. Most successful enterprises find some way to share the wealth, and what is a dividend if not a profit-sharing plan? Wiping out a century of enmity between capital and labor will be hard to do, perhaps impossible, but that reality does not obviate the basic underlying truth that employees (and investors generally) should be able to take advantage of the publicly traded status of our most successful companies in this country to own at least a small stake in them.

The list of possible objections to Kelso's plan is long. In theory employees can already purchase stakes in their dividend-paying companies in the open market, but encouraging broader ownership is likely to involve issuing new shares to them, probably at a discount. Doing so would be dilutive to existing company owners. And if share repurchase programs are scaled way back—as they should be—that would mean that the share counts at many U.S. corporations would rise, perhaps materially. But encouraging share ownership among all employees likely to be with the firm for a long period is clearly a good idea, even if that means that the share count would grow in parallel. Second, despite what Kelso wrote, some corporations simply cannot and should not pay material, if any, dividends. (Cue the airlines, many retailers, and materials companies.) And companies need to avoid paying excessive dividends. In the late 1960s, the Penn Central railroad continued making cash distributions even when the profits underpinning those distributions weren't there. The company ended up in bankruptcy. In the most recent financial crisis, too many banks were paying dividends up until they disappeared in arranged marriages or simply failed. Forcing companies to pay dividends when they shouldn't is not the point. Rather, with the payout ratio of the S&P 500 Index companies at 30%, there are just far too many major U.S. corporations that can afford a dividend but do not have one, or have one that is grossly insufficient.

Taxation is another objection. Dividends are paid from after-tax profits. In contrast, paying someone a higher wage or a year-end bonus is a tax-deductible expense. Distributing excess company profits as a dividend therefore is a lot less efficient than just paying it as compensation. I don't dispute the tax argument but would argue that the benefits of having more employees see themselves and comport themselves as company owners offsets the greater expense of a dividend-based profit-sharing plan.

Rather than try to resurrect Kelso's specific vision, my goal is simply to point out the undesirable condition of mistrust and the below-optimal stock ownership level that has become accepted as normal in this country. Refocusing the attention of corporate America on dividends will not on its own resolve the existing misalignment of incentives, but it would represent an acknowledgment of the problem and an attempt to address it.

(Double) Taxation

I ended *The Strategic Dividend Investor* with an afterword on taxes. The rules were changing as the book went to print, and there was no time to integrate the material into the text. Two years later, the exact same situation holds. The ultimate outcome in regard to the taxation of dividends is unclear, but we can be certain of one thing: rates are going up. It's not certain by how much and for whom, but they are going up. In the previous afterword, I made the point that *investors* need to realize that the after-tax advantages of going for capital gains only pale in comparison to the total return advantage of dividend-oriented portfolios. That is, the risk of doing a lot worse by trying to "buy low, sell high, repeat frequently" is not worth saving a percent or two due to higher tax rates on dividends. Two years later, that argument is unchanged for individual investors, but the present work is targeted as much to the *dividend payers*, corporate America. In a rising tax environment, these entities might be tempted to do some tax planning on behalf of company owners by shifting cash from a taxable dividend stream to "rewarding" shareholders with share repurchase programs that would facilitate—it is hoped—capital gains taxable only at the time of sale. Please do not bother. Corporations are not owned in order to provide tax advice, and as I have tried to illustrate, this effort at tax planning fails miserably. An income stream that is taxed more highly is still going to be worth more to company owners than a lower income stream, one where the dividend has been reduced and the funds redirected to the stock market where they essentially disappear. For instance, a $1.00 dividend taxed at 15%—the rate through 2012—at least leaves $0.85 in the pockets of company owners. But if the dividend is lowered, say by 25% to $0.75, and the difference is used for share repurchases, the situation is quite different. In theory, if many factors work in favor of the repurchase plan, the share count will decline and the value of an individual share will rise by some amount. And the shareholder can sell his or her stake into the market and use the money to find another income stream. Maybe that will work out if the timing is not too bad and the transaction costs are not too high and a myriad of other factors don't get in the way. But one thing is certain: the original income stream has been impaired. Not only is $0.75 a lot lower than the starting $1.00 dividend, but after taxes are paid, only $0.64 makes it to the company owner. That share repurchase program *had better work*, because in addition to enduring the burden of double taxation (discussed below), the company owner has to accept an even greater decline in the income stream due to management's decision to "help" shareholders on the tax front.

From a public policy perspective, higher levels of taxation on dividend income may increase the revenue in the government's coffers but at the cost of punishing those who invest for dividends in favor of those who speculate in share prices for capital gain only. Rather than encourage more broad-based dividend investment, higher taxation on dividend income pushes people in exactly the wrong direction, toward trying their hand at guessing the movement of share prices. Rather than bring more dividends to Main Street, that will just generate more trading profits on Wall Street.

Let me finish with a bold and what some would consider a political statement: taxes on dividend income aren't low, they are exceptionally high. What gets lost in the discussion of dividend taxation is the basic, undeniable fact that the profits that are distributed in this country as dividends are taxed twice, first at the corporate level (where there is a statutory rate of 35%) and then again at the investor level (at whatever the marginal rate for that individual may be). It adds up to a stunning amount of taxation. Let's say Acme Widget has $100 in pretax income and 10 shareholders with equal stakes. That translates into $10 per share of taxable profits. Like most U.S. corporations, Acme does some planning around its taxes and gets the effective rate down to 30%. So net income per share for Acme is now $7.00. For the past decade, the tax rate on dividend income has been 15%. Applying that tax rate takes the per share after-tax cash ultimately received by each owner down to $5.95. So even in the "low" dividend tax environment that we have enjoyed during the past decade, the effective rate on dividend income has been around 40%.

In small businesses, partnerships, and other investment structures (such as real estate investment trusts, or REITs), the profits are not taxed at the company level but are "passed through" to the company owner, so they are taxed only once.

In those instances, one can argue the merits—both economic and social—of various levels of individual taxation, but that is not the case for most investors in most public companies for whom the income stream is taxed twice. Ownership of a stake in a major, publicly traded corporation, rather than direct ownership of a business that might have that "pass-through structure," offers certain advantages, it is true, but does the desire to hold stock in large American enterprises justify the penalty of double taxation? I would say no.

Conclusion

My conclusions are straightforward: investors should assess their stock market holdings as they would any other business undertaking. Money may be placed in high-risk, potentially high-return start-up ventures, or it may be put in mature and stable cash distributive enterprises. If it is the former, certain expectations apply. By definition, the wager is going to be speculative. If it works out, perhaps at some distant time in the future, the company will be able to make steady cash distributions to the owners. Or the stake can be sold to someone else who sees worth in those future cash distributions. In the meantime, it is a "trade," not a long-term investment. There is nothing wrong with having a "trade" or even a lot of them in one's portfolio, as long as the stakeholder understands that fact and does not confuse it with a long-term investment.

But if the company in question is a mature, ongoing enterprise, it should be able to make cash distributions, the present value of which is equal to or perhaps even greater than the current price for that business. If that present value is lower than the current price, then you have a problem. In making an effort to understand your business investments and where they fall out, focus on the cash you actually receive, not the "malarkey" that comes out of Wall Street (and alas from the companies themselves). There may have been a time when simply tracking a company's earnings could help one come to a solid, long-term investment decision, but that time is long past. Diluted earnings, quarterly earnings, normalized earnings, earnings before charges, beat by a penny—these are the rogue characters in a bad, made-for-TV drama. Have as little to do with them as possible. Focus on the cash. The value of that cash and the trajectory of it will give you the best glimpse as to the value of the business to other investors—the stock price. If the distributions are rising, the share price will as well. If they are falling, expect the share price to follow. If they are moving sideways, settle in for the wait.

Over the past several decades, corporate America has been shifting money away from the dividends that drive positive net present value and redirecting the cash to share repurchase programs and large-scale M&A that do not. It's time for that to stop. Why? Because the result of the Great Retreat is a basic Finance 101 problem. From a simple NPV perspective, it's hard if not impossible to justify an investment offering a 2% yield, growing at just around 5%, and offering a roller-coaster ride of volatility. That's the U.S. stock market currently.

Not only does the low-yield, low-payout "new normal" not make sense from a financial math perspective, it has also contributed, along with many other factors, to the alienation of corporate America—increasingly conflated with Wall Street—from Main Street. Unmoored from cash dividend payments, stocks are now just pieces of paper of tremendously uncertain value. They used to represent ownership stakes in companies known for their goods and services and backed by tangible, distributed cash flows that testified to the company's real-world success. In the absence of that cash flow, it's no wonder that investors no longer trust the stock market and no longer see the companies behind the stocks. Corporate America can help itself here simply by putting some cash back into the ownership proposition. Perhaps then more employees and more of Main Street would be inclined to take a stake in and find themselves identifying with, and not against, our country's most successful businesses.

Endnotes

Chapter 1

1. Irving Fisher, *The Nature of Capital and Income* (New York: Augustus M. Kelley, 1965 reprint of 1906 original), p. 188.
2. The DCF formula is: $PV = E \times (1 + G)/(R - G)$ where PV is present value (or price you would be willing to pay), E is profits, G is the long-term growth rate of those profits, and R is the discount rate. Make the growth rate 0 (zero), and the formula simplifies to $PV = E/R$. If you move the E over, the P/E equals 1 over the discount rate.
3. FactSet Research Systems and Federated Investors, 2012, as of November 27, 2012. Out of 3,726 securities, 52.5% were without dividends. A similar analysis of the Russell 3000 Index showed 50.9% without dividends.
4. FactSet Research Systems and Federated Investors, as of December 31, 2011.
5. There is no single standard for companies taking charges. This chart is based on Compustat's definition of Unusual Expenses as calculated by Société Générale Cross Asset Research. Assessments of charges from other sources show similarly high percentages for the past decade.
6. FactSet Research System, using Compustat data, 2012, for data from 1990 through 2011. It is possible companies could have an unusual expense and an unusual gain in the same year of the same amount, in which case they would show as having no unusual net expense for that year. The likelihood of that happening frequently is quite low.
7. There are individual quarters when S&P 500 operating earnings are lower than reported earnings, but no calendar-year measurement periods when that is the case.

8. FactSet Research Systems and Federated Investors, 2011.
9. Aswath Damodaran, *The Little Book of Valuation* (Hoboken, NJ: John Wiley & Sons, Inc., 2011.), p. 197.
10. FactSet Research Systems and Federated Investors, 2012.
11. In Table 1.4, the group of 13 eliminators is combined with the 4 continuous non-payers. The median total return for this larger group is 7.0%. The overall cohort calculations do not account for spin-offs prior to 1984. Data sampling suggests that in frequency and magnitude, such spinoffs were insignificant.
12. Cohorts of 1962, 1970, and 1980 are all companies for which continuous data was available. Cohorts for 1990 and 2000 are drawn from top 1,500 and 2,000 companies, respectively. For all cohorts, a security must be a primary issue, must be a common stock, cannot be an American Depositary Receipt (or similar), must be denominated in U.S. dollars, and must be domiciled in America. The price and dividend of the security must be available during the entire period. Any member of an earlier class is automatically included in all subsequent classes, regardless of size.

Chapter 2

1. For financial firms, the path to free cash flow is a different one than for nonfinancials and can be generally approximated by net income plus amortization charges. The free cash flow figures used here are a combination of traditional free cash flow from nonfinancials added to net income plus amortization charges from companies in the financial sector.
2. In the interest of simplification, I've ignored any interest that the cash on the balance sheet might be generating. That would be lost when the cash balance is drawn down. In the current, structurally low interest rate environment, it is not a factor.
3. www.sec.gov/rules/final/33-8335.htm.
4. For instance, Pankaj N. Patel, "Share Buybacks and Beyond," Credit-Suisse Quantitative Analysis, Equity Research, June 19, 2012.
5. Michael Mauboussin, "Share Repurchase from All Angles," *Perspectives*, Legg Mason Capital Management, June 2012, p. 2. Emphasis in original.
6. John Boris, "Has PFE's Share Repurchases Created Shareholder Value?," *Citi Investment Research & Analysis*, May 29, 2012.
7. Warren Buffett puts it succinctly: "If stock options aren't a form of compensation, then what are they? If compensation is not an expense, then what is it?"
8. FactSet Research Systems and Federated Investors, 2012.

9. William J. Bernstein and Robert D. Arnott, "Earnings Growth: The Two Percent Dilution," *Financial Analyst Journal*, September–October 2003, pp. 47–55.

10. "The Negative Side of Share Buybacks," Reuters Breakingviews commentary by Robert Cole and Quentin Webb, *New York Times*, August 25, 2011, p. B2.

11. Twelve-month data from November 28, 2011, to November 27, 2012, from FactSet Research Systems and Bloomberg L.P.

12. FactSet Research Systems and Federated Investors, 2012.

Chapter 3

1. FactSet Research Systems and Federated Investors, 2012. Data for 460 companies. The other 40 did not have 10-year independent sales data. Most were either new corporations or spin-offs that did not exist independently a decade earlier. An adjustment was made to the growth rate of certain utilities to account for a change in revenue recognition during the measurement period. This change did not affect the median result.

2. www.data360.org.

3. Companies reporting a loss for 2011 are excluded from the scatterplot.

4. The plot excludes the five companies that lost money in the past year but still had a dividend.

5. Poornima Gupta, "HP's 2013 outlook Disappoints, Shares Near 9-Year Low," Reuters, October 3, 2012.

6. The math adds up if you consider H-P's share issuance, debt issuance, sale of businesses, and the drawdown of cash on hand.

7. You will notice that IBM's dividend, acquisitions, and repurchases exceed the amount of free cash flow. That is because the company has also issued $9.3 billion in stock in the same period.

8. As of September 30, 2012. Some of this cash represents amounts held outside the United States. Apple would incur a tax payment were it to repatriate those funds. Company owners still "own" that cash, however, and avoiding taxes is an insufficient reason for management to deprive owners of their rightful assets.

9. "JT Rebuffs Calls for Dividend Increase," *Financial Times*, April 26, 2012.

10. Imperial Tobacco demerged from Hanson Industries and began trading independently in 1996. Century-old BAT was separated from BAT Industries and began trading as a pure tobacco company in 1998. Reynolds Tobacco (later renamed Reynolds American) was split off from RJR Nabisco and began trading as a pure tobacco

company in 1999. Altadis was purchased by Imperial Tobacco. The initial bid was announced in March 2007. Gallaher Group was purchased by Japan Tobacco. The initial bid was announced in December 2006.

11. Bloomberg, L.P., 2012. Data for the S&P 500 Index.

12. That is now seven, as one, American Tower (AMT) has since reorganized itself into a REIT and has been categorized as a financial.

13. Some readers might wonder whether the 30% dividend payout ratio limit on major financials is an important factor in the market's overall low payout ratio. It is not. That ratio has been coming down for decades. Having all the major U.S. financial institutions get stripped of their dividends in 2008 and 2009 did not help matters much—the dividend for the S&P 500 Index fell from a peak of $29 per unit of the index in 2007 to $21 in early 2009—but keep in mind that the contribution of the financials to the profits of the index also fell sharply, so much so that with all the write-offs, S&P 500 Index reported profits fell from a peak of $81.51 per unit of the index in 2006 to $14.88 in 2009. In fact, the payout ratio temporarily surged. So, no, the low payout ratio is not just a consequence of the financials being knocked out of the equation.

Chapter 4

1. A small number of major publicly traded companies are still family or founder controlled. As such, they fit within the owner-operator model, and for them, splitting the role of chairman and CEO would make little sense.

2. You can read about the certificate, a joint venture of Pearson Education and the *Financial Times* (owned by Pearson) at: www.non-execs.com/certificate (website content reviewed as of July 2012).

3. Having options where the strike price is adjusted for dividend payments would achieve the same goal.

4. Aronson v. Lewis, 473 A.2d 805, 812 (Delaware, 1984). Approximately 60% of S&P 500 Index companies are incorporated in the state of Delaware.

5. You can read the original ruling online: www.businessentitiesonline.com/Dodge%20v.%20Ford%20Motor%20Co.pdf.

6. Louis O. Kelso and Patricia Hetter, *How to Turn Eighty Million Workers into Capitalists on Borrowed Money* (New York: Random House, 1967), pp. 77–78.

Index

Abbott Laboratories, 36, 133
"Adjustments," to earnings, 20–21, 32
ADRs (American Depository Receipts or Shares), 85
Agency cost, 142–144
Altadis, 116–117
Altria Group, 117
Amazon, 88, 118
American Depository Receipts or Shares (ADRs or ADSs), 85
Annual total return, 42
Apple Inc., 9, 37–39, 72–73, 76, 88, 94, 104–106
aQuantive, 16–17
AT&T Inc., 94, 131
Avon, 124–125

Baby boomers, 128, 156
Balance sheet efficiency, 68–70
Bank of America Corp., 30, 37, 58, 94, 103–104
Berkshire Hathaway Inc., 94, 97–98, 104
Bloomberg, 20–21, 22
Board of directors, 142–173
   agency cost and, 142–144
   balancing act with employees, 164–170
   business judgment rule, 161–162

chief executive officer (CEO) and, 145–150, 151–152, 160
dividend payout ratio and, 143–145, 147–148, 150–161, 163–164
economic growth and, 155–156
employee stock ownership plans and, 164–170
independent directors, 147
interest rates and, 145, 152–156
mergers and acquisitions and, 157–159
relationship between owners and operators, 142–144
responsibility of, 149, 151–152
scandals and, 144, 150, 165, 166
share repurchases and, 148, 150, 152–153, 156–157
taxation of dividends and, 170–173
trust in, 161–173
Boeing, 76
Bristol-Myers Squibb, 133
British American Tobacco, 117
Buffett, Warren, 97–98, 104
Business judgment rule, 161–162

in consumer discretionary,
130, 131–132
in consumer staples, 130, 131
declining, 37–39, 142–144
determining correct levels,
129–135
in energy, 95–96, 104, 130,
132–133
executive compensation linked
to dividend growth,
160–161
in financials, 32, 103–104,
130, 131–132
by global industry sectors,
130–135
gross domestic product versus,
87
in health care, 130, 132–133
historic trends, 9, 37–39, 89–93,
125–129, 142–144
in industrials, 130, 131–132
in information technology,
98–103, 104–106, 130,
134–135, 165–166
in materials, 130, 131
sales growth rates and, 86–88
by S&P 500 global industry
classification, 130–135
in telecommunications, 130–131
in utilities, 130, 131, 153–154
Dividend yield, 40, 41–42
Dutch East India Company, 141

Earnings
"adjustments" to, 20–21, 32
compensation of managers
and, 70
dilution. *See* Dilution of
earnings
dividend growth, 10–11, 40
earnings growth, 10–11
estimated, 25–27, 28, 30, 39
in financial service companies,
30–31
forecasting, 32
increased debt and, 68–71

normalized, 14–25
number of shares outstanding
and, 51–53
operating versus reported,
18–20
quarterly estimates versus
annual reports, 28, 39
share repurchase impact on,
51–53, 61–71
timing of earnings reports,
27–30
Eastman Kodak, 37
eBay, 37–39
EBITDA (earnings before interest,
taxes, depreciation, and
amortization), 6
Economic growth, 87–88,
105–106, 150–151, 155–156
Eli Lilly, 133
Employee stock ownership plans,
164–170. *See also* Stock
options
Energy company dividend payout
ratios, 95–96, 104, 130,
132–133
Enron, 144, 165
Equity risk premium, 111–114
ExxonMobil Corp., 94, 95–96,
133

FactSet Research Systems, 20–22
FASB (Financial Accounting
Standards Board), 18–19
Financial engineering, 71, 135–136
Financial service companies
dividend payout ratios, 32,
103–104, 130, 131–132
earnings reports, 30–31
injustices of, 80
Fisher, Irving, 1, 42
Ford, Henry, 162
Ford Motor Company, 94, 103, 162
Forecasting
bias in, 73–74
dividend, 32
Foreign corporations, 86, 114–118

About the Author

Daniel Peris was educated at Williams College, the University of Oxford, and the University of Illinois at Urbana-Champaign from which he received a Ph.D. in History. Peris was a Fulbright-Hays Scholar in the former Soviet Union in 1991–1992 and is the author of a book and several articles on modern Russian history. Since 2002, he has worked at Federated Investors in Pittsburgh where he is a Senior Portfolio Manager. In addition to *The Dividend Imperative*, Peris is also the author of *The Strategic Dividend Investor* (McGraw-Hill, 2011).

For more information, please visit:
www.dividendimperative.com